DATE DUE

MAJOR WORLD LEADERS

Pervez Musharraf

Sara Louise Kras

CHELSEA HOUSE
PUBLISHERS
A Haights Cross Communications Company

Philadelphia

CHELSEA HOUSE PUBLISHERS

V.P., New Product Development Sally Cheney
Director of Production Kim Shinners
Creative Manager Takeshi Takahashi
Manufacturing Manager Diann Grasse

Staff for PERVEZ MUSHARRAF

Executive Editor Lee Marcott
Senior Editor Tara Koellhoffer
Production Assistant Megan Emery
Picture Research 21st Century Publishing and Communications, Inc.
Series and Cover Designer Takeshi Takahashi
Layout 21st Century Publishing and Communications, Inc.

A Haights Cross Communications ◂ Company

http://www.chelseahouse.com

First Printing

1 3 5 7 9 8 6 4 2

Library of Congress Cataloging-in-Publication Data

Kras, Sara Louise.
   Pervez Musharraf / by Sara Louise Kras.
      p. cm.—(Major world leaders)
Includes index.
Summary: A biography of the Pakistani president, from childhood to his current position
of power, acquired in a military coup
   ISBN 0-7910-7650-4 (Hardcover)
   1. Musharraf, Pervez. 2. Pakistan—Politics and government—1988– 3. Presidents—
Pakistan—Biography. [1. Musharraf, Pervez. 2. Presidents—Pakistan. 3. Pakistan—
Politics and government—1988–] I. Title. II. Series.
DS389.22.M87K73 2003
954.9105—dc21

                                                                    2003009494

TABLE OF CONTENTS

On Leadership

Arthur M. Schlesinger, jr.

Leadership, it may be said, is really what makes the world go round. Love no doubt smoothes the passage; but love is a private transaction between consenting adults. Leadership is a public transaction with history. The idea of leadership affirms the capacity of individuals to move, inspire, and mobilize masses of people so that they act together in pursuit of an end. Sometimes leadership serves good purposes, sometimes bad; but whether the end is benign or evil, great leaders are those men and women who leave their personal stamp on history.

Now, the very concept of leadership implies the proposition that individuals can make a difference. This proposition has never been universally accepted. From classical times to the present day, eminent thinkers have regarded individuals as no more than the agents and pawns of larger forces, whether the gods and goddesses of the ancient world or, in the modern era, race, class, nation, the dialectic, the will of the people, the spirit of the times, history itself. Against such forces, the individual dwindles into insignificance.

So contends the thesis of historical determinism. Tolstoy's great novel *War and Peace* offers a famous statement of the case. Why, Tolstoy asked, did millions of men in the Napoleonic Wars, denying their human feelings and their common sense, move back and forth across Europe slaughtering their fellows? "The war," Tolstoy answered, "was bound to happen simply because it was bound to happen." All prior history determined it. As for leaders, they, Tolstoy said, "are but the labels that serve to give a name to an end and, like labels, they have the least possible connection with the event." The greater the leader, "the more conspicuous the inevitability and the predestination of every act he commits." The leader, said Tolstoy, is "the slave of history."

Determinism takes many forms. Marxism is the determinism of class. Nazism the determinism of race. But the idea of men and women as the slaves of history runs athwart the deepest human instincts. Rigid determinism abolishes the idea of human freedom—the assumption of free choice that underlies every move we make, every word we speak, every thought we think. It abolishes the idea of human responsibility, since it is manifestly unfair to reward or punish people for actions that are by definition beyond their control. No one can live consistently by any deterministic creed. The Marxist states prove this themselves by their extreme susceptibility to the cult of leadership.

More than that, history refutes the idea that individuals make no difference. In December 1931 a British politician crossing Fifth Avenue in New York City between 76th and 77th Streets around 10:30 P.M. looked in the wrong direction and was knocked down by an automobile— a moment, he later recalled, of a man aghast, a world aglare: "I do not understand why I was not broken like an eggshell or squashed like a gooseberry." Fourteen months later an American politician, sitting in an open car in Miami, Florida, was fired on by an assassin; the man beside him was hit. Those who believe that individuals make no difference to history might well ponder whether the next two decades would have been the same had Mario Constasino's car killed Winston Churchill in 1931 and Giuseppe Zangara's bullet killed Franklin Roosevelt in 1933. Suppose, in addition, that Lenin had died of typhus in Siberia in 1895 and that Hitler had been killed on the Western Front in 1916. What would the 20th century have looked like now?

For better or for worse, individuals do make a difference. "The notion that a people can run itself and its affairs anonymously," wrote the philosopher William James, "is now well known to be the silliest of absurdities. Mankind does nothing save through initiatives on the part of inventors, great or small, and imitation by the rest of us—these are the sole factors in human progress. Individuals of genius show the way, and set the patterns, which common people then adopt and follow."

Leadership, James suggests, means leadership in thought as well as in action. In the long run, leaders in thought may well make the greater difference to the world. "The ideas of economists and political philosophers, both when they are right and when they are wrong," wrote John Maynard Keynes, "are more powerful than is commonly understood. Indeed the world is ruled by little else. Practical men, who believe themselves to be quite exempt from any intellectual influences, are usually the slaves of some defunct economist. . . . The power of vested interests is vastly exaggerated compared with the gradual encroachment of ideas."

But, as Woodrow Wilson once said, "Those only are leaders of men, in the general eye, who lead in action. . . . It is at their hands that new thought gets its translation into the crude language of deeds." Leaders in thought often invent in solitude and obscurity, leaving to later generations the tasks of imitation. Leaders in action—the leaders portrayed in this series—have to be effective in their own time.

And they cannot be effective by themselves. They must act in response to the rhythms of their age. Their genius must be adapted, in a phrase from William James, "to the receptivities of the moment." Leaders are useless without followers. "There goes the mob," said the French politician, hearing a clamor in the streets. "I am their leader. I must follow them." Great leaders turn the inchoate emotions of the mob to purposes of their own. They seize on the opportunities of their time, the hopes, fears, frustrations, crises, potentialities. They succeed when events have prepared the way for them, when the community is awaiting to be aroused, when they can provide the clarifying and organizing ideas. Leadership completes the circuit between the individual and the mass and thereby alters history.

It may alter history for better or for worse. Leaders have been responsible for the most extravagant follies and most monstrous crimes that have beset suffering humanity. They have also been vital in such gains as humanity has made in individual freedom, religious and racial tolerance, social justice, and respect for human rights.

There is no sure way to tell in advance who is going to lead for good and who for evil. But a glance at the gallery of men and women in MAJOR WORLD LEADERS suggests some useful tests.

One test is this: Do leaders lead by force or by persuasion? By command or by consent? Through most of history leadership was exercised by the divine right of authority. The duty of followers was to defer and to obey. "Theirs not to reason why/Theirs but to do and die." On occasion, as with the so-called enlightened despots of the 18th century in Europe, absolutist leadership was animated by humane purposes. More often, absolutism nourished the passion for domination, land, gold, and conquest and resulted in tyranny.

The great revolution of modern times has been the revolution of equality. "Perhaps no form of government," wrote the British historian James Bryce in his study of the United States, *The American Commonwealth*, "needs great leaders so much as democracy." The idea that all people should be equal in their legal condition has undermined the old structure of authority, hierarchy, and deference. The revolution of equality has had two contrary effects on the nature of leadership. For equality, as Alexis de Tocqueville pointed out in his great study *Democracy in America*, might mean equality in servitude as well as equality in freedom.

"I know of only two methods of establishing equality in the political world," Tocqueville wrote. "Rights must be given to every citizen, or none at all to anyone . . . save one, who is the master of all." There was no middle ground "between the sovereignty of all and the absolute power of one man." In his astonishing prediction of 20th-century totalitarian dictatorship, Tocqueville explained how the revolution of equality could lead to the *Führerprinzip* and more terrible absolutism than the world had ever known.

But when rights are given to every citizen and the sovereignty of all is established, the problem of leadership takes a new form, becomes more exacting than ever before. It is easy to issue commands and enforce them by the rope and the stake, the concentration camp and the *gulag*. It is much harder to use argument and achievement to overcome opposition and win consent. The Founding Fathers of the United States understood the difficulty. They believed that history had given them the opportunity to decide, as Alexander Hamilton wrote in the first Federalist Paper, whether men are indeed capable of basing government on "reflection and choice, or whether they are forever destined to depend . . . on accident and force."

Government by reflection and choice called for a new style of leadership and a new quality of followership. It required leaders to be responsive to popular concerns, and it required followers to be active and informed participants in the process. Democracy does not eliminate emotion from politics; sometimes it fosters demagoguery; but it is confident that, as the greatest of democratic leaders put it, you cannot fool all of the people all of the time. It measures leadership by results and retires those who overreach or falter or fail.

It is true that in the long run despots are measured by results too. But they can postpone the day of judgment, sometimes indefinitely, and in the meantime they can do infinite harm. It is also true that democracy is no guarantee of virtue and intelligence in government, for the voice of the people is not necessarily the voice of God. But democracy, by assuring the right of opposition, offers built-in resistance to the evils inherent in absolutism. As the theologian Reinhold Niebuhr summed it up, "Man's capacity for justice makes democracy possible, but man's inclination to justice makes democracy necessary."

A second test for leadership is the end for which power is sought. When leaders have as their goal the supremacy of a master race or the promotion of totalitarian revolution or the acquisition and exploitation of colonies or the protection of greed and privilege or the preservation of personal power, it is likely that their leadership will do little to advance the cause of humanity. When their goal is the abolition of slavery, the liberation of women, the enlargement of opportunity for the poor and powerless, the extension of equal rights to racial minorities, the defense of the freedoms of expression and opposition, it is likely that their leadership will increase the sum of human liberty and welfare.

Leaders have done great harm to the world. They have also conferred great benefits. You will find both sorts in this series. Even "good" leaders must be regarded with a certain wariness. Leaders are not demigods; they put on their trousers one leg after another just like ordinary mortals. No leader is infallible, and every leader needs to be reminded of this at regular intervals. Irreverence irritates leaders but is their salvation. Unquestioning submission corrupts leaders and demeans followers. Making a cult of a leader is always a mistake. Fortunately hero worship generates its own antidote. "Every hero," said Emerson, "becomes a bore at last."

The signal benefit the great leaders confer is to embolden the rest of us to live according to our own best selves, to be active, insistent, and resolute in affirming our own sense of things. For great leaders attest to the reality of human freedom against the supposed inevitabilities of history. And they attest to the wisdom and power that may lie within the most unlikely of us, which is why Abraham Lincoln remains the supreme example of great leadership. A great leader, said Emerson, exhibits new possibilities to all humanity. "We feed on genius. . . . Great men exist that there may be greater men."

Great leaders, in short, justify themselves by emancipating and empowering their followers. So humanity struggles to master its destiny, remembering with Alexis de Tocqueville: "It is true that around every man a fatal circle is traced beyond which he cannot pass; but within the wide verge of that circle he is powerful and free; as it is with man, so with communities." ■

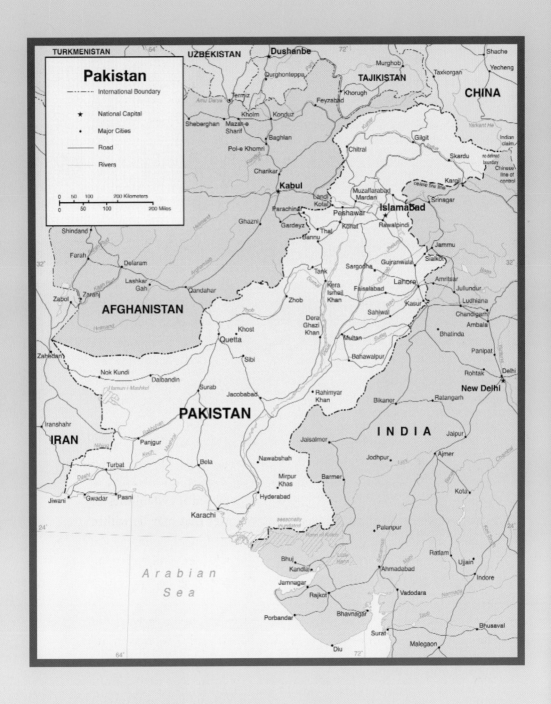

1

A Daring Move

I n October 1999, General Pervez Musharraf was about to make a very daring move. Law and order in Pakistan were in a crisis. The foreign debt of the Muslim country was at an all-time high, $32 billion. Public opinion of Prime Minister Nawaz Sharif had plummeted.

The reasons behind Musharraf's bold move began a couple of months earlier. This was when the Pakistani army, led by Musharraf, finally had an advantageous position in the continuing battle against India for control of the Kashmir area. The army was about to achieve a significant victory. However, pressured by the United States, Sharif ordered a complete withdrawal from Kashmir. This decision led to a secret plot by Musharraf and the army commanders to overthrow the Pakistani prime minister.

It took Pakistan's military only 17 hours to execute a coup on the

Pervez Musharraf (right) greets former Prime Minister Nawaz Sharif (left) as Sharif arrives in Kali, a town in the disputed Kashmir region. This photograph was taken a month after Sharif was deposed by Musharraf's military forces in October 1999.

government. It began early on a Tuesday afternoon, October 12, 1999. Musharraf, the chief of army staff, was out of the country for an official visit to Sri Lanka, an island country south of India. He was set to fly back at 2:45 P.M. on Flight 805 on Pakistan International Airlines with an estimated time of arrival in Karachi at 6:55 P.M. There were 197 other passengers on the plane.

Sharif had plans of his own regarding Musharraf. He had decided to replace Musharraf as his chief of army staff while Musharraf was out of the country. He knew that Musharraf was headed back to Pakistan so he ordered traffic control to stop Flight 805 from landing. Then he quickly made an official announcement on Pakistani television that Musharraf had been retired and had been replaced by Lieutenant General Khwaja Ziauddin. While flying home, Musharraf had no idea what was happening in Pakistan. He was relaxed on the flight and was busy sifting through papers and preparing for a meeting the next day with Sharif.

After the TV announcement of Musharraf's retirement, the country's top military officials quickly held a one-hour meeting and decided to strike back against the prime minister. They spurred their troops toward Islamabad, the capital of Pakistan. Within 90 minutes, 3,000 soldiers poured onto the streets of the capital. Soldiers began to take control of government buildings and then shut down all television broadcasts.

By 6:30 P.M., the first group of soldiers reached the prime minister's house. The soldiers quickly secured the gatehouse and headed toward the main entrance. On the porch was Ziauddin, the proposed new chief of army staff, with six Inter-Services Intelligence officers. The soldiers threatened them with rifles. Ziauddin and the officers backed down. Inside was the prime minister. The soldiers told him that he needed to step down from his political post, but he refused.

At the airport, the managing director of Pakistan International Airlines took over the control tower to stop Musharraf's plane from landing in Pakistan. When the plane tried to land, the pilot was refused permission. The pilot told the tower that the plane was soon going to run out of fuel. He was told to land in a neighboring country. The pilot said, "But the only country for which we have fuel is India." "Then land in India," was the cocky reply.

The pilot remembered the incident later: "I advised Karachi Air Traffic Control that I had 198 souls on board, a limited amount of fuel, and that if we were not allowed to land we would lose the aircraft and that would be the end of the story."

Musharraf had no idea what was happening in the cockpit until the pilot summoned him. He entered the cockpit and was immediately told that the plane was not allowed to land in Pakistan. Musharraf took control of the radio, told the tower that he was on the plane, and ordered the tower to allow the plane to land since it was running out of fuel. The people in the tower still refused permission to land. To stop the plane from landing, police trucks blocked the runway and the landing lights were switched off.

Musharraf managed to get a phone line to one of his army captains in Pakistan and was told about the military action then under way. The captain told the general that he would secure the airport so his plane could land. The control tower was surrounded by the military, and the plane was finally allowed to touch down. Once the plane landed, the pilot checked the fuel gauges on the plane and saw that the aircraft had only seven minutes worth of fuel left. Later, in a speech to the country, Musharraf said, "Thanks be to Allah, this evil design was thwarted by the speedy army action."

At 10:15 P.M., TV broadcasts were restored. Within 15 minutes, an announcement ran across the bottom of the screen stating that Prime Minister Nawaz Sharif had been dismissed. At 2:50 A.M., an announcer stated that General Pervez Musharraf would address the nation to explain why the military had to take control. The people of Pakistan breathed a sigh of relief that Sharif was no longer in power.

Musharraf's early military experience helped to shape him

On October 17, in the immediate aftermath of his successful coup, Pervez Musharraf addressed the Pakistani people on television. He assured Pakistanis that the military forces that had taken control of the nation would only rule until an appropriate civilian government could be put into place.

into a man who could overthrow a corrupt, democratically elected government. Today, he is described as a soldier's soldier and carries himself like a "battle-hardened commando." To fully understand the brazen leader of Pakistan, one must return to the past to see the events that made him what he is today.

Pervez Musharraf was born on August 11, 1943, behind a cinema in Daryaganj, Delhi. He was born in a *haveli*. These were large mansions with many rooms; kings and queens used to live in them years ago, but they later became huge living spaces for families. At the time of his birth, his father was a cashier with the Directorate General of Civil Supplies in Delhi. Both of Musharraf's parents were educated. His mother received a master's degree in English literature at Delhi's Indraprastha College. His father graduated from Aligarh University. A devout Muslim, he had nearly memorized the entire Koran.

The first four years of Musharraf's life were happy while he lived in the haveli. He was the second of three sons born to a Syed family. The Syed line is supposed to be composed of families with bloodlines traced to Muhammad, the Prophet of Islam. The Syed line is the highest level of the Islamic caste system of distinct social classes.

When Musharraf was born in 1943, India was under British rule and included what is now Pakistan and Bangladesh; the nation of Pakistan did not exist. Before 1945, all Indians, including Hindus, Sikhs, and Muslims, put aside their religious differences to fight for one cause—the release of India from British rule.

Once the people of India saw that victory would be theirs, problems began to develop between the Hindus and Muslims. The Muslims felt that the Hindus would treat them unjustly once India became its own country. The Muslims wanted India to be a Muslim country, but the Hindus and Sikhs had no intention of letting that happen. The confusion turned into violence.

India was given its independence on August 14, 1947. But beforehand, mass upheaval and bloodshed had started to break out among the three main religious groups: Hindus, Sikhs, and Muslims, all of which had very different beliefs.

Hindus worship Brahma, the creator of the universe, and believe in a strict caste system that separates people into distinct social classes. People of one caste cannot have social dealings with people of another caste. Also, in the Hindu religion, the cow is considered sacred and is not eaten. It is sacred because of its gentle nature and because it provides milk, which makes butter, cheese, and yogurt.

The Hindus and Sikhs live in relative peace. The Sikhs are a Hindu sect, a small group that has broken away from a larger religion. They believe in one god and do not practice the caste system. Sikh men believe they must never cut their hair, and they always wear a beard. A man's hair is tied into a large knot on top of his head and covered with a turban. Sikhs believe in the teachings of the ten gurus, which are in the Sikh Holy Book. A guru is a spiritual advisor or teacher. There is a living guru today, who is like a prophet of the Sikhs.

The Muslim religion believes that there is one god, called Allah, and that Muhammad is his prophet. Part of the Muslim religion includes frequent prayer. There are five prayer sessions that must be performed daily.

Because of their wide differences, Muslims and Hindus had frequent battles. Before Pakistan was created and Muslims and Hindus all lived in India, Muslims would deliberately offend Hindus by slaughtering a cow in front of them. In turn, Hindus would hold noisy celebrations during the Muslims' time of worship.

The Muslims wanted a separate country from the Hindus and Sikhs, and so Pakistan was created. It originally had two parts—an eastern section and a western section. The western section is the Pakistan of today. The eastern section fought for independence from Pakistan in 1971 and is now known as Bangladesh. The word *Pakistan* means "Land of the Pure." The separation of India and Pakistan into independent nations is referred to as the Partition.

Within a few days of Pakistan's coming into existence, the Hindus, Sikhs, and Muslims started to kill each other. It was as if a civil war were taking place, despite the Partition's effort to avoid one. Villages were burned to the ground. Women and children were kidnapped or murdered. Hundreds of

When the Partition of 1947 divided the nations of India and Pakistan, violence broke out between opposing Muslims and Hindus. To escape the chaotic situation in independent India, many thousands of Muslims fled their former homes to live in the newly created state of Pakistan.

thousands of people began to flee; Hindus and Sikhs to India, and Muslims to Pakistan. The Partition caused the migration of 12 million people. At the end of the chaos, hundreds of thousands of people had been killed. The Partition and the subsequent violence was a huge human catastrophe for India and Pakistan. Even to this day, the violence that occurred has left an enormous scar on these two countries.

Even though Musharraf was only four years old at the time, this event affected him for the rest of his life. In 1947, Musharraf's father gathered the family together to prepare to leave India for Pakistan. They had no time to take any possessions from their house. His father boarded them on the last train from Delhi to Karachi, Pakistan, a journey that would take three days. The train was completely packed with people. Passengers were even hanging from doorways and sitting on top of the train, tied down with their bundles. Inside, the heat was intolerable because it was summer. Making all of this worse, there was no food or water on the train.

During the journey, the family was terrified that Hindus and Sikhs would stop the train. As they moved quickly along the tracks, the view from the window was horrifying. Smoke filled the air as villages and neighborhoods burned. Dead bodies lay along the train tracks. Years later, when Musharraf was asked what he remembered about the terrible train ride, he said, "A lot of tension. A lot of worry. A lot of fear."

Musharraf also remembered that his father had carried a little metal box while on the train. He had been asked by the new Pakistani government to protect Pakistan's share of the foreign ministry's funds and to deliver the funds to Karachi. Musharraf recalled, "He was guarding this little box with his life. He used to sleep with his head on it. And when he was awake, he'd sit on it."

The move to Pakistan separated Musharraf for many years from his uncles, aunts, and cousins who remained in India. Almost 50 years would pass before he would meet them again.

Once the Musharraf family arrived in Pakistan, they were received as immigrants, or *mohajirs*. His father began working for the Pakistan Foreign Service.

The new nation of Pakistan had many obstacles to

overcome, even more than India. It had no capital city and no government buildings. Since Pakistan had not existed before, all the government files and records for the region were in New Delhi, India, which had been the British capital for many years. All government services like roads, the postal system, the railway system, and dams had been built for one nation, not two.

One of the biggest problems, which Pakistan and India still face today, is the status of Kashmir and Jammu. These large states lie in the east of Pakistan and in the north of India. They are in mountainous areas that lie between Afghanistan, China, Tibet, and the former Soviet Union. The two regions are lush and extremely beautiful, featuring lakes with hand-carved houseboats floating on them, picturesque gardens, green fields, and fruit orchards.

All the rivers that flow through Pakistan begin in Kashmir. Pakistan uses these rivers for an irrigation system that provides water for 33 million acres of land. This is another reason why this area is so important to Pakistan and its people.

When the British withdrew from India, 562 states had to decide which country to join, Pakistan or India. During this time, the majority of people in Kashmir and Jammu were Muslim. Even so, they were ruled by a Hindu maharajah or prince. Most states quickly made their choices, but the ruling maharajah of Kashmir and Jammu put off deciding which country to join for two months. Secretly, the maharajah was hoping that somehow Kashmir and Jammu could become a separate country entirely. While he was deciding what to do, Muslims within Kashmir revolted against his rule. They started to set up their own government and asked the new country of Pakistan to come to their aid. The maharajah had nowhere else to turn but India. He asked India's help against the Muslim rebels. India brought troops into Kashmir, and the Pakistanis were driven back to what is now known as the Line of Control. This is a 450-mile (724-kilometer) separation line that has been agreed

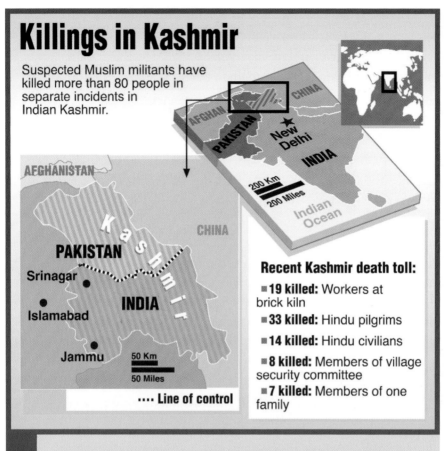

Killings in Kashmir

Suspected Muslim militants have killed more than 80 people in separate incidents in Indian Kashmir.

New Delhi

INDIA

CHINA

AFGHAN

PAKISTAN

200 Km

200 Miles

Indian Ocean

AFGHANISTAN

PAKISTAN

Srinagar

Islamabad

Jammu

INDIA

CHINA

Kashmir

50 Km

50 Miles

•••• Line of control

Recent Kashmir death toll:

- **19 killed:** Workers at brick kiln
- **33 killed:** Hindu pilgrims
- **14 killed:** Hindu civilians
- **8 killed:** Members of village security committee
- **7 killed:** Members of one family

The region of Kashmir has been in dispute ever since India and Pakistan were created in 1947. Both countries believe they are the rightful rulers of Kashmir, and bloody wars have been fought through the years as Indians and Pakistanis have attempted to assert their authority over the area. This map shows the location of the controversial region, and also outlines some of the violence that has taken place.

upon by Pakistan and India. It divides the positions of the Pakistani army and the Indian army in Kashmir.

After India assisted the maharajah, it claimed the Kashmir area once the maharajah signed an Instrument of Accession to India. This document declared that Kashmir and Jammu agreed to the dominion of India. Even though Kashmir and Jammu would rule themselves, they were still connected to India by defense, currency, foreign affairs, and communications.

Pakistan did not agree to or acknowledge this document. Instead, the government of Pakistan felt that its fellow Muslims in Kashmir needed to be liberated from Hindu rule.

To settle the dispute over Kashmir and Jammu, the United Nations passed a resolution in 1948. It stated that Pakistan was to completely withdraw from Kashmir and Jammu, which never happened. India was to reduce its troops to a minimal amount, which it never did. Once Pakistan and India took those steps, a vote called a referendum was to be monitored by the international community. The referendum would allow the people of Kashmir and Jammu to decide which country they would join. The referendum never materialized. Without the agreement of Pakistan, India had claimed Kashmir as its territory. Pakistan's reason for existence was to provide a homeland for Muslims in the India-Pakistan area. Because of the large Muslim population in Kashmir, Zulfikar Ali Bhutto, later to become Pakistan's president, said in 1964, "Kashmir must be liberated if Pakistan is to have its full meaning."

Even today, Pakistan blames India and India blames Pakistan for the battles that have taken place in Kashmir. The fight to control Kashmir and Jammu goes on. The battle to free Kashmir must have made quite an impression on young Musharraf. To this day, he demands time and time again that the Kashmir issue must be resolved.

In 1949, Musharraf's father was transferred to Ankara, Turkey, to work at the Pakistani Embassy. Musharraf was six years old when the family moved there. His family remained in Turkey for seven years.

Musharraf recalled, "When I was a child in Turkey, . . . we had two defense attachés who used to wear these beautiful glamorous uniforms. I used to look at them, and I was extremely impressed by their smartness. That was the time I also thought, I must wear such uniforms."

Mustafa Kemal Ataturk, who was Turkey's president from 1923 to 1938, was one of his heroes. Later in life, Musharraf listed Kemal Ataturk as the person he most admired on his official profile. Musharraf remembered, "I was strongly attracted to Kemal Ataturk's model of leadership. He transformed Turkey from being the 'sick man of Europe' to being a very advanced nation."

Kemal Ataturk can be described as the father of Turkish secularism, separating religion from government. To a degree, Musharraf has also fashioned his political party today the same way. He has kept the strong Muslim religious groups in check by flexing his military power.

Coming from a family of government workers, young Musharraf was the only member interested in joining the army. He knew at an early age that he wanted to become a soldier. His mother encouraged Musharraf's decision. She had a vision for her three boys. Musharraf remembered his mother telling him, "I would go to the army, my elder brother would become a civil servant, and my younger brother, a doctor." All of these dreams came true.

While Musharraf lived in Turkey, he became fluent in the Turkish language under the guidance of a German tutor. It is rumored that even today he is able to speak, read, and write Turkish better than Urdu, the official language of Pakistan.

In 1956, Musharraf moved back to Karachi, Pakistan. There he received a very diverse education. He attended St. Patrick's High School and then went on to attend Forman Christian College in Lahore.

In high school and college, Musharraf was an average student. He had a strong passion for sports. He loved to play tennis and also enjoyed water sports like canoeing and sailing. His favorite subject was military history. Being an avid reader, he became very knowledgeable on the subject.

He never wavered in his decision to become a military man. Once Musharraf finished his schooling, he immediately joined the Pakistan Military Academy and then advanced steadily from one position to another up through the military hierarchy.

2

Rapid Advancement in the Military

I n 1961, Musharraf enrolled in the Pakistan Military Academy, located at Kakul. When he went to the school, he shifted his permanent residence to the city of Gujranwala, which is in a northeastern Punjab province. He also declared this city to be his hometown, possibly so he could erase his roots in India and the label of being a mohajir.

This decision would assist him in his future military career and any possible political career. Because 70 percent of the officers in the Pakistani army are Punjabis, mohajirs do not often advance well within the ranks. And it is impossible to separate military and political careers within Pakistan, since during Pakistan's short history as a nation, military governments have ruled for more than 25 years.

Musharraf was at the military academy from 1961 to 1964. When

Seen here after he had become a well-respected general, Pervez Musharraf got his start in the army when he attended the Pakistan Military Academy as a young man. The lessons he learned there would serve him well as he went on to fight for and eventually lead his country.

he graduated, he was 20 years old. The arduous training in the Himalayan foothills hardened Musharraf. In the military academy's yearbook, one of Musharraf's classmates wrote in his entry about Musharraf: "Quite a guy to be with, especially when in a fix."

He graduated second in his class and joined the 16th field artillery regiment as a second lieutenant, a commissioned officer of the lowest rank. He was promoted to lieutenant and saw combat within a year in the Indo-Pakistan War. The battle took place in an area called Punjab, which is in northeast Pakistan and northwest India. Musharraf's battery, a basic unit of artillery or mounted guns such as cannons, was bombarded by Indian artillery. His post was heavily hit and was soon ignited by the shellfire. Even so, Musharraf refused to leave his position. Because of his bravery, he was decorated with a medal called Mention in the Dispatches. Musharraf believed his escape from death during this battle was a miracle.

Musharraf continued his military career by volunteering to be transferred for seven years to the Special Services Group (SSG) in 1966. This group was made up of the Pakistani army's irregular warfare unit.

The SSG was a commando unit, or a small group of soldiers trained to make surprise raids into enemy territory. These units consisted of 32 to 94 soldiers. In Mary Anne Weaver's book, *Pakistan: In the Shadow of Jihad and Afghanistan,* she states, "The commando unit had only recently been raised, in a joint undertaking of the Pakistani Army and the Special Forces of the United States. At this point . . . Musharraf began forming a bond with the United States." The SSG was similar to the U.S. army's special unit called the Green Berets.

Musharraf turned out to be tough, courageous, and willing. He was trusted, and therefore, was sent to the most difficult battles against India. The SSG motto was: "Who Dares, Wins." "I was always a risk taker," remembered Musharraf, who trained his men not to flinch at danger. He soon gained a reputation as a brilliant field tactician, a person who understands the science of maneuvering military forces in battle to gain the advantage. He had much practice at this while fighting India. Even so, his army friends did not think he was very good at strategic thinking, the science of planning large-scale military operations. Instead, all he pursued throughout his adult life was the battle against India, mostly in the limited realm of the Kashmir area.

While in the SSG, Musharraf was promoted to captain. With this rank, he was placed in charge of the Kamal company of the SSG. He was involved in many reconnaissance missions to find out information about the enemy position. The reconnaissance missions that the Kamal company executed were against India's communication lines.

Meanwhile, in his personal life, Musharraf married Begum Sehba on December 28, 1968. Even though Sehba was a Muslim, she was not a fundamentalist, which meant she did not adhere to strict Islamic law. She has been photographed many times without a scarf. A traditional Muslim woman wears a scarf called a *hijab* that covers her head, neck, and ears. Musharraf held beliefs similar to his wife's, so he had no objections. They went on to have two children, a son and a daughter.

Musharraf considered himself a moderate Muslim. He allowed himself to have an occasional drink of scotch whiskey before dinner, and he occasionally indulged in gambling. A devout Muslim would never have done either. Musharraf had been influenced by his boyhood contact with Christian missionary schools. He asserted himself as an avowed secularist.

In his military career, he continued to advance. Musharraf served as a major from 1971 to 1973. This was a fast promotion and quite impressive. His unit, the 2nd battalion of the SSG, was based in eastern Pakistan to fight the 1971 war that broke out between West Pakistan and East Pakistan. East Pakistan wanted its independence. It would be renamed Bangladesh and received military support from India.

The specialty of Musharraf's unit was to destroy any installments like bridges and roads, and to commit acts of terrorism. There were rumors of shocking war crimes committed by Musharraf's unit, but there was no proof to back up the allegations. During this time, the other Pakistani forces in the battle against eastern Pakistan collapsed, and the soldiers in Musharraf's unit had to run for their lives. Meanwhile, 93,000 Pakistani soldiers had surrendered to India.

At the end of 1973, Musharraf was scheduled to go on leave, but an avalanche at his post caused him to delay his departure. Later, Musharraf found out that the plane he was scheduled to take for his leave had crashed, killing everyone on board. He believes this was a second miracle that allowed him to escape death.

From 1973 to 1979, Musharraf attended the Command and Staff College in Quetta and the National Defense College. After his education, he was promoted to lieutenant colonel.

During much of this period, Pakistan's prime minister was Zulfikar Ali Bhutto. Bhutto worked to lead the country toward democracy. He founded the Pakistan People's Party and began land reforms. A dialogue was also established with India because of Bhutto's efforts.

A political crisis broke out in Pakistan in 1977, and General Muhammad Zia-ul-Haq placed Bhutto in prison. The general then put Pakistan under martial law on July 5, 1977. Within two years, General Zia-ul-Haq had Bhutto tried in the Supreme Court. He was found guilty and sentenced to death. On April 4, 1979, Bhutto, the former democratic leader, was hanged, and General Zia-ul-Haq took on the title of chief martial law administrator.

At this time, the U.S. government had great interest in the stability of Pakistan. Factors outside of Pakistan caused the United States concern. In Iran, the ruling shah had been exiled,

Musharraf was on friendly terms with Pakistani General Mohammed Zia-ul-Haq (seen here). This relationship helped Musharraf advance politically after Zia-ul-Haq overthrew Prime Minister Zulfikar Ali Bhutto in 1977 and took over the government himself.

and a religious leader, Ayatollah Khomeini, took control of the country. Saudi Arabia began to be a major power in the Middle East, and the Soviet Union began to invade Afghanistan. With these events, ensuring stability in Pakistan was a high priority

Part of Musharraf's job in the early 1980s was to help prepare the *mujaheddin*, or Muslim holy warriors, who fought to remove the Soviets from Afghanistan. These mujaheddin soldiers are resting in the Kunar Province region of Afghanistan in May 1980.

for the United States in order to protect Western sources of oil in the Middle East.

In 1979, Musharraf became friendly with General Zia-ul-Haq. The ruling general discovered that Musharraf was a fellow mohajir. Because of this, he chose Musharraf for advancement in his political circle. Several martial law administration offices were set up throughout Pakistan. Musharraf was appointed to run a district martial law administration headquarters.

Between 1979 and 1985, Musharraf became involved in preparing the fighters in Afghanistan called *mujaheddin*, who were battling the Soviet Union. The Central Intelligence Agency (CIA) was also involved in supplying these fighters with weapons and money.

American analyst Selig Harrison later said, "The CIA made a historic mistake in encouraging Islamic groups from all over the world to come to Afghanistan. The U.S. provided $3 billion for building up these Islamic groups, and it accepted Pakistan's demand that they should decide how this money should be spent."

Pakistan was responsible for setting up training schools called *madrasas*. These schools were used to teach Islamic beliefs, provide military training, and plan the transportation and supplies needed for the covert war against the Soviets in Afghanistan. They were heavily funded by Pakistan, Iran, and other Arab states.

In the madrasas, children learned the Koran by heart and were taught not to question the Muslim religion. They learned that virtue lay in unthinking obedience. As the children got older, they were shown how to use hand weapons, and they received instructions on making and planting bombs. The more promising students were sent to specialized secret army camps, which became the training area for Afghanistan's Taliban. Recruits were pulled from the student bodies of the madrasas. Originally set up as religious schools, they eventually became a place to preach the Taliban's militant ideas for *jihad*, or holy war. As a result, the 2,500 madrasas produced about 225,000 Islamic fanatics who were prepared to kill and die for the Muslim religion. All it took was an order by one of their religious leaders.

It is highly possible that Musharraf may have come in

contact with Osama bin Laden, the leader of the terrorist organization Al Qaeda, at this time. Bin Laden was involved in finding recruits and money to funnel into the madrasas. There are also reports that Musharraf had contact with drug smugglers in the area.

According to J. Arya of Pakistan-Pacts.com, because of Musharraf's connection to the United States at this time, "it is also suggested that Musharraf secretly attended at least one course at the Green Berets training school at Fort Bragg. Accounts indicate Musharraf's performance in these courses was above average."

Musharraf was later promoted to deputy director of military operations. This position was responsible for coordinating the different operations of the Pakistani army. The army's directing staffs decided, too, on the best route to train future soldiers and officers. Drills were created to prepare officers on how to deal with various military situations. Holding this post allowed Musharraf to establish the very essence of the Pakistani military's philosophy.

From 1985 to 1987, Musharraf was encouraged by General Zia-ul-Haq to put together a Special Snow Warfare Force. With the new unit, Musharraf launched an attack on an Indian post at Bilafond Pass in Kashmir.

This area is one of the world's harshest environments. It has frozen rivers of ice, deep crevasses, unpredictable avalanches, and freezing, howling winds. During the summer the temperature inches up to -35° C (-31° F), and in the winter it dips down to -69° C (-92° F).

Musharraf's force successfully captured two Indian army posts. General Zia-ul-Haq was pleased with Musharraf's work and rewarded him. Musharraf became the Pakistani army's top mountain warfare expert.

In retaliation, the Indian army sent its own mountain warfare expert, Brigadier General Chandan S. Nugyal, to the Bilafond Pass. As a result, the Indian army retook its lost posts from the Pakistani army. To this day, Pakistan has never acknowledged the defeat on Bilafond Pass. As Arya put it, "Visiting dignitaries are often shown the peak and told that it is a Pakistani held position."

Musharraf was establishing himself as a valuable army officer. Through his various endeavors, he had met men who would further assist him in the future.

3

Making a General

I n May 1988, Musharraf requested the help of Osama bin Laden. He asked that tribesmen from Afghanistan, led by bin Laden, be transported to fight the Shiites in Gilgit, Pakistan. The Shiites were demanding an independent state.

Shiite Muslims are a minority in Pakistan. Sunni Muslims are the majority. The difference between the two is the Shiites' belief that Ali, the son-in-law and cousin of Muhammad, the Prophet of Islam, was the first *imam*. An imam is a Muslim priest who recites prayers and leads worship. It is also believed that Ali was the true successor to the Prophet Muhammad. The Sunnis believe that the first four caliphs, or supreme rulers, were the rightful successors of the Prophet Muhammad. Because of the two groups' different beliefs over who was Muhammad's successor, arguments and violent acts sometimes break out between them.

Pervez Musharraf was a talented military tactician who was also well respected by the men he led. Here, a Pakistani soldier who fought against Indian troops in Kashmir embraces the famous general (left).

With the help of bin Laden's spare men and a Pakistani Special Services Group unit, the revolt by the Shiites was suppressed. Pakistani newspapers reported that Musharraf's troops invaded the area. They destroyed houses and crops and killed a large number of Shiites. To stifle any future revolts,

Musharraf started a policy of bringing in people from other ethnic and religious groups to lessen the numbers of Shiites living in the Gilgit area. The policy is still practiced today.

This same year, Pakistan's dictator, General Zia-ul-Haq, considered Musharraf to become the military secretary. Instead, another man was selected. Within a few weeks, the general and his new military secretary died in a plane crash. Musharraf believed that this was the third time he had miraculously escaped death.

During 1989 and 1990, Musharraf commanded an artillery unit. He also was a deputy military secretary and a member of the War Wing of the National Defense College. At this time, he was quoted during an interview as saying, "It would be insane to attack India via the Siachin [Glacier]. It would make more sense to attack at a more southern point closer to their lines of communication." This comment could have been the seed to planning his famous attack on Kargil in 1999.

Musharraf then took a course at the Royal College of Defense Studies in England, where he graduated with a master's degree. It was at this time, 1990 and 1991, that concern about the nuclear weapons race between Pakistan and India first appeared in Musharraf's dialogue. He did a research project titled, "Impact of the Arms Race in the Indo-Pakistan Subcontinent."

He was an excellent student, and the commanding officer of the school described him as, "A capable, articulate and extremely personable officer, who made a most valuable impact here. His country is fortunate to have the services of a man of his undeniable quality."

Musharraf returned to Pakistan in 1991 and was promoted to major general. The war against the Soviet Union in Afghanistan was ending, so the trained mujaheddin no longer had a war to fight. The government of Pakistan thought it would be a good idea to use these soldiers to fight the battle in Kashmir.

The merger between the Pakistani army and the mujaheddin

soon proved to be unsuccessful, as the different mujaheddin groups began to fight each other. Also, India soon arrested three of their major leaders. Because of the terrorist techniques these groups used, like kidnapping civilians, and their ties to Osama bin Laden, the United States officially labeled them as terrorist organizations in 1997.

From 1993 to 1995, Musharraf was the director general of military operations. During this time he was prominent in the program that monitored the conduct of the Taliban in Afghanistan. The Taliban's aim was to bring order to a country filled with chaos after many years of war with the Soviet Union and internal tribal warfare. Pakistan was involved with Taliban activities to ensure that it held some control over the new governing group in Afghanistan.

Pakistan provided the Taliban with finances, weapons, and military equipment via its Inter-Services Intelligence. The Taliban received support through air force pilots and army units used to direct the government group's efforts. Pakistan also supplied continuous recruits from its madrasas.

Assisting the Taliban was supposed to help Pakistan by bringing in money from Middle Eastern countries to fund the madrasas in Pakistan. Instead, all it did was bring international alienation.

Musharraf was promoted to lieutenant general on October 21, 1995. The chief of army staff was General Jehangir Karamat. Whenever General Karamat traveled overseas, Musharraf was appointed acting chief of army staff.

In 1997, Nawaz Sharif was elected prime minister of Pakistan. He had been prime minister in 1990 but was dismissed in 1993. After Sharif's second election, Musharraf began courting him to be promoted to chief of army staff.

Even though Sharif had sought out election to be prime minister, it was rumored that he really did not have much interest in politics. He only ran for office because his father wanted a political influence to protect his various businesses.

After Nawaz Sharif became prime minister of Pakistan in 1997, Musharraf tried to win himself a position within the new government. His efforts succeeded. The prime minister (right) appointed Musharraf (left) to be army chief of staff.

After his election, Sharif definitely had his hands full with Pakistan's many internal problems. Adult literacy in Pakistan was only 40.9 percent; children under the age of five were underweight compared with those in other countries; almost half of the Pakistani people did not have proper sanitation; and inflation was at an all-time high, with many people living in poverty.

Regardless of these issues, Sharif had plans of his own. Reminded of his dismissal in 1993, he wanted to make sure his political position remained completely secure. He first attacked the free press. Newspaper editors who printed negative articles against him were harassed and investigated for tax evasion. He weakened Parliament by forcing an amendment to the constitution stating that all members of Parliament must vote according to the policy followed by the current political party. The Supreme Court tried to bring him under control and ordered him to appear before it because of a contempt of court case filed against him. Sharif organized a mob of supporters that interrupted Supreme Court proceedings by smashing furniture. The Supreme Court judge was terrified and backed down. Even though his actions were harsh, Sharif became a national hero in May 1998 when his administration executed the first atomic bomb testing in Pakistan.

Under Prime Minister Sharif, Musharraf witnessed a dramatic change in the capabilities of the Pakistani army. Musharraf had become very familiar with the military landscape of Pakistan through the positions he held and the battles he had fought. Even so, the year 1998 would bring a powerful new military tool that would soon be at his disposal. Pakistan was soon to be among the countries with nuclear capabilities.

4

Pakistan and the Nuclear Bomb

Pakistan's nuclear program started with a member of the Pakistani government, Zulfikar Ali Bhutto. As early as 1965, Bhutto made the famous comment: "If India builds the bomb, we will eat grass or leaves, even go hungry, but we will get one of our own."

In 1965 came the first big step toward nuclear capabilities for Pakistan. Canada had agreed with the Pakistani government to build a nuclear power plant outside of Karachi. By 1972, the plant was creating electricity via nuclear energy and plutonium, which had military possibilities. However, Pakistan did not have complete control of the plant. To operate it successfully, Pakistan needed the assistance of Canadian experts and parts.

In 1969, Bhutto argued that Pakistan had to acquire a nuclear bomb to match the progress being made in India. He wrote,

One of the most pressing issues in the often hostile relationship between Pakistan and India has been the possession of nuclear weapons. In 1965, Zulfikar Ali Bhutto (seen here), who later became prime minister, said that Pakistan would work hard to develop its own bomb if India successfully created a nuclear weapon.

"If Pakistan restricts or suspends her nuclear program, it will not only enable India to blackmail Pakistan with her nuclear advantage, but would impose a crippling limitation on the development of Pakistan's science and technology."

In December 1971, Zulfikar Ali Bhutto became Pakistan's president and was later appointed prime minister. From 1971 to 1977, he headed the Atomic Energy Commission. Even so, Pakistan's weapons program had to be executed in complete secrecy. Bhutto was considered the architect and designer of

Pakistan's nuclear policy. He felt that there should be a nuclear bomb to protect Islam.

In January 1972, Bhutto held a secret meeting with Pakistan's top scientists and military officers. During this meeting, Bhutto announced his intentions to develop a nuclear bomb within three years. Pakistan began to set up facilities for this purpose. The project became known as Project 706 and was supervised by Bhutto.

In the middle of negotiating the purchase of a reactor fuel reprocessing plant from France, Pakistan's nuclear plans were frustrated. France signed the Treaty on the Non-Proliferation of Nuclear Weapons and stopped the sale of the plant to Pakistan. The treaty's purpose was to prevent the spread of nuclear weapons and weapon technology, and instead, pursue peaceful ways to use nuclear energy. The treaty was first opened for signature in 1968 and was in force by 1970. Currently, more than 187 parties have signed the treaty, but Pakistan and India have not. Five countries that have signed have nuclear weapons.

Even though there were setbacks for Pakistan in pursuing its nuclear objectives, a talented Pakistani scientist, Dr. A.Q. Khan, soon entered the picture and became the key to making the atomic bomb for Pakistan a reality. He had worked in Belgium and Germany for 15 years. During this time, he had learned how to enrich uranium to levels necessary to build a bomb. In 1974, he proposed to the Pakistani government that the route to an atomic bomb was to pursue uranium enrichment technology. Khan was put to work on the project.

Pakistan's concerns about defending itself were truly realized when India conducted its first nuclear bomb test in 1974. Nuclear weapons being made in abundance in unauthorized nations soon became an international fear. Pakistan felt this fear when in 1977, the Canadian government decided that its nuclear plant in Karachi did not have enough security and cut off all supplies for nuclear fuel.

Even so, Pakistan's pursuit of nuclear weapons did not stop. Secret negotiations still occurred through skilled Pakistani agents and middlemen in Europe. Components were bought on the sly around the world from countries like Sweden, Germany, and the United States. Somehow the secret purchases were discovered. Top Pakistani scientists, including Khan, were judged around the world and found guilty. Warrants were out for their arrest.

Even though restrictions were tight, the Pakistani government posted more special agents in Europe and the Far East. Some worked at the Pakistani embassies, and some started fake companies. The agents were to continue purchasing items used to make a nuclear bomb. If the agents were caught with the items, they would say that the items were for civilian use, not military. Western governments tried very hard to catch the agents in the act but seemed to be always one step behind them.

In 1976, U.S. Secretary of State Henry Kissinger visited Prime Minister Bhutto. He told him that if Pakistan halted its nuclear pursuits, the United States would furnish him with political support. Bhutto refused and later called it a bribe. When Bhutto turned down the secretary of state's offer, in Tariq Ali's book, *The Clash of Fundamentalisms, Crusades, Jihads and Modernity*, he states, Bhutto received a warning from Kissinger: "We can destabilize your government and make a horrible example out of you."

Within six months, these words came true. Bhutto was removed by a political coup. He had to face trial, was found guilty, and within two years was executed.

The United States issued sanctions in April 1979 against Pakistan because it continued pursuing a nuclear bomb under the new government. Sanctions are actions, such as blocking shipped goods to a country, that are taken by a group of nations against another nation that is considered to have broken international law.

In 1981, however, the United States would need Pakistan's assistance to fight the Soviet Union in Afghanistan. The sanctions against Pakistan were lifted, and the Pakistani nuclear program took a backseat to more pressing issues. Pakistan was offered a $3.2 billion aid package in exchange for its help in fighting the Soviet Union in Afghanistan.

Pakistan continued its secret nuclear program and, in 1984, Khan announced his success in enriching uranium. The purpose of the enriched uranium was solely to create a nuclear bomb. Even so, outside of Pakistan, Khan stated that there were other purposes. He issued several statements saying he was appalled that the international community would think the enriched uranium was for military purposes. Instead, he said, it was for peaceful uses.

Much later, in May 1998, when Pakistan first conducted atomic bomb testing in the Chagai Hills, Khan confidently stated, "I never had any doubts. I was building a bomb. We had to do it." Within Pakistan, Khan became a national hero.

In a CNN interview that month, Khan contended that Pakistan could mount a nuclear bomb on a medium-range missile within a matter of days. "The nuclear devices which we have tested are very compact. They can easily be connected to weapons if the need arises. So we wanted to convey the message that no one should be under any illusion that these are crude and clumsy devices." He claimed that the medium-range missile could travel up to 1,000 miles (1,609 kilometers) and could be fired without detection. Pakistan now felt confident that India would think more than twice about invading it.

Immediately after nuclear testing in Pakistan, Prime Minister Sharif declared an emergency and suspended all fundamental rights. Western countries and Japan were imposing heavy sanctions. Even though Pakistan had greatly assisted the United States during the crisis in Afghanistan, sanctions had again been placed on Pakistan as soon as the conflict was over. These sanctions hit hard on the country's economy, which was already failing. Pakistan's economy deteriorated further with skyrocketing prices, increased unemployment, and ineffective law enforcement.

Pakistan successfully tested its first nuclear weapon, the Ghauri-II missile, in May 1998. A month later, Pakistani scientist Abdul Qadeer Khan (at podium) addressed a large crowd as the people celebrated the new missile's inauguration.

Musharraf was bitter about the disloyal behavior of the United States. When asked by Mary Anne Weaver what he felt the United States should do for Pakistan, she stated in her book, *Pakistan: In the Shadow of Jihad and Afghanistan*, that he replied, "The United States must help clean up the mess that you created during the days of the Soviet occupation of Afghanistan. Pakistan served your interests. . . . But when the Soviets withdrew, the U.S. government also pulled out, leaving us high and dry."

Even though the Western world disapproved, both Pakistan and India fully justified their nuclear capabilities. The purpose was to create a preventive measure against a nuclear attack by their enemy.

A good example of this came during the Kargil invasion in 1999. India felt embarrassed because it had not seen the approaching Pakistani troops, and the government discussed crossing the border into Pakistan and starting a war. Another idea was to cross into Pakistan and demand negotiations. India finally resorted to using international pressure on Pakistan to withdraw. Even so, the possibility of using a nuclear bomb was in the background.

During the Kargil conflict, one senator on the Pakistan Defense Committee questioned why Pakistan had made nuclear bombs in the first place if they were not going to be used. He felt one of Pakistan's bombs should be dusted off and sent on its way to India.

A senior advisor to India's prime minister said, "We will not be the first to use nuclear weapons. But if some lunatic tries to do something against us, we are prepared."

Prime Minister Sharif was concerned that the conflict might lead to a nuclear war that could completely destroy both countries. This real threat hanging over both countries may have been the reason negotiations were possible.

Pakistan's nuclear capabilities increased the chance of an Asian holocaust, which could happen three different ways. The first way was demonstrated by the close call from the Kargil incident: Both countries would deliberately decide to use the nuclear bomb to solve their disputes. The second way would be a human blunder that would release an atomic bomb, starting a war by accident. The third way would be a war started when unauthorized people obtained access to atomic bombs and set them off. Each country has to maintain a system of checks and balances to keep its arsenal of atomic bombs secure.

Making a nuclear bomb a reality for Pakistan was a dream come true for Khan, the government, and the army. There is little information about Musharraf's connection to the nuclear program during this period. Because of his high-ranking position in the army, though, it was highly possible he had something to do with the nuclear decisions. He may have even been asked to approve the nuclear bomb tests held in Chagai Hills.

Pervez Musharraf, a diligent leader of soldiers, was witnessing changing military power and alliances within Pakistan. After arranging a meeting with Sharif, Musharraf put himself forward as a possible successor to the chief of army staff. Sharif saw Musharraf as potentially loyal and subservient, qualities sought by a prime minister who was losing patience with all who opposed him. Musharraf would not have to sit very long in the wings before he found himself in the most coveted military position, the chief of army staff.

5

Tensions Build Between Sharif and Musharraf

Prime Minister Nawaz Sharif had just fired his chief of army staff for speaking out about the poor performance of the Sharif government. The economy was failing, and violence was spreading among the various ethnic groups. Sharif seemed to be doing nothing to resolve these important issues. The chief of army staff criticized this, saying he felt Sharif and his advisors should include the army in their decision-making. Angered by these comments, Sharif eliminated him and needed to quickly replace him with someone who could be controlled and was liked by the army men. The army rejected his first choice, Khwaja Ziauddin. Pervez Musharraf became a middle-ground choice. So, on October 7, 1998, he was appointed general and chief of army staff.

Musharraf was considered a modest man who had a calm voice and an air of seriousness about him. Army men liked and respected

Pervez Musharraf (center) became the chief of army staff in Prime Minister Nawaz Sharif's government (Sharif is seen second from left) after the army rejected the first candidate Sharif suggested. Both the army and the prime minister agreed that Musharraf was a good choice because he was talented, serious, and well liked by enlisted men.

him, and Sharif felt that he was not a threat. He could not have been more wrong. Because Sharif had fired the previous chief of army staff, Musharraf was alerted to Sharif's impulsive nature. Musharraf continuously watched his back and kept an eye on the prime minister. He was wary of the leader, who was trying to control everyone around him.

Neighboring India was not too happy with the appointment of Musharraf as the chief of army staff. India was suspicious of Musharraf's motives and intentions because of his warlike past toward India. Officials there considered him too ambitious and linked to many Islamic fundamentalist groups.

Musharraf immediately went to work with Sharif. He helped restore law and order in Karachi, which was very violent at the time. The army was also assigned to conduct a census to count all the people and sort them by age, sex, and occupation. Another duty of the army was to collect bills for the Water and Power Development Authority. Musharraf willingly took on these extra duties.

Musharraf asserted that he was not afraid to face challenges. He had no idea of what lay ahead, however. Little did he know that after being handpicked by Sharif, the prime minister would eventually get tired of Musharraf and try to get rid of him, too.

In the beginning of 1999, Washington, D.C., was pressuring Sharif and Musharraf to set up a special commando unit to enter Afghanistan and capture Osama bin Laden. The unit was established even though Musharraf was not very enthusiastic about the idea. But the unit never set out for Afghanistan. Instead, a U.S. intelligence officer discovered that Pakistan was sharing several military training camps with bin Laden's group, Al Qaeda.

Meanwhile, Sharif extended an invitation to the prime minister of India, Shri Atal Behari Vajpayee, to visit Pakistan on February 20, 1999. Sharif arranged to have a banquet that evening in honor of Vajpayee at the Lahore Fort to formally celebrate the first public use of bus service from Lahore, Pakistan, to New Delhi, India.

The next day, the two leaders discussed several mutual and international issues and came up with the following conclusions: They both agreed to meet occasionally to discuss nuclear-related concerns, and agreed that the system of visas between the two countries needed to be relaxed. In addition, a committee was to be appointed to examine humanitarian issues concerning civilians who had been detained and missing prisoners of war.

Both sides expressed approval of the new bus line and setting up the release of civilian detainees. On February 21, 1999, the prime ministers signed the Lahore Declaration, which said that they shared visions of peace and stability between the two countries. It also outlined their hope for progress and prosperity for the citizens of Pakistan and India.

Musharraf was not excited about the Lahore Declaration. While the meeting was taking place, he was making plans to invade India. Within just a few months, all of Sharif's supposed hopes for peace with India would be dashed by a rash move made by the Pakistani army, known as the Kargil incident—an incident that would make Sharif and Musharraf's relationship come to a head in the spring of 1999.

During the continuous war over Kashmir, Pakistan and India had an informal agreement that the two armies would not occupy high points in Kargil from September 15 to April 15 each year because of the extreme weather conditions. In order to attack, the Pakistani army made the decision to ignore the agreement. This was the perfect time to gain more control in the Kashmir area.

In the snowy peaks of the Himalayan Mountains in Kashmir, Musharraf gave his troops the order to cross the Line of Control. This line was agreed upon by Pakistan and India to separate their armies' position. Musharraf's 1,500 soldiers advanced toward the Kargil ridges. Some soldiers rode snowmobiles, and some climbed through the deep snow to this most strategic position in Kashmir. They

The issue of control over Kashmir has led to violence many times throughout the short history of India and Pakistan. In this July 1999 photograph, Pakistani soldiers are firing at Indian army positions in the Kargil sector of Kashmir.

brought equipment to climb mountains and supplies for the battle. The soldiers continued toward Kargil. The objective was to cut off roads and an important Indian communications network. When the Indian forces returned later in the spring, they found Pakistani soldiers occupying the Kargil heights.

The town of Kargil was caught in the middle of tremendous crossfire between the Pakistani and Indian armies. Shopkeepers closed up their stores, and people ran for cover. The people most hurt by the continued battle over Kashmir were those who lived there. All they really wanted was independence, but instead two foreign armies occupied their land. These armies belonged to countries that neither spoke Kashmir's language nor understood its worries.

The Pakistanis were definitely at the advantage because of their position in the Kargil heights. The Kargil incident was a military success. Even so, after six weeks of warfare with India, Pakistan had lost about 700 soldiers.

Pakistan was in a position to force India to create new agreements. India complained loudly to the international community, and Prime Minister Sharif found himself in an international crisis. Sharif resented the move by the Pakistani army and complained, "General Musharraf had marched his men to the top of the hill without considering how he would get them down."

On the weekend of July 4, the White House sent for Sharif. President Bill Clinton told Sharif to withdraw the Pakistani troops from the Kargil area. There were no negotiations. Sharif was not promised anything for doing this, and no pressure had been exerted on India. Sharif gave up without a fight and agreed. The prime minister indicated to Clinton that he wanted friendly relations with India and had resisted the idea of the Kargil invasion. Regardless, the army had proceeded without the agreement of the head of government in Pakistan.

When Sharif returned to Pakistan, he ordered the military troops to withdraw from Kargil to keep international peace. This decision caused resentment among the army ranks, and Sharif was labeled a coward.

It was the final straw when, in Washington, Sharif passed the blame to Musharraf for the Kargil incident. The army officers suspected that Sharif's intelligence agency had bugged Musharraf's conversations with his righthand man, Lieutenant General Muhammad Aziz. They also believed that Sharif handed the tapes over to government officials in New Delhi, India.

Musharraf was furious that Sharif would go to Washington and not even consult him on the terms of withdrawal. The defense committee of the cabinet had been meeting to decide on a cease-fire and had not reached an agreement when Sharif decided to go to Washington.

Musharraf made an announcement that everyone in the Pakistani government had been on board with the Kargil attack. He further said that he refused to withdraw. Meanwhile, Sharif signed an agreement with the United States to withdraw from Kargil. To say that Musharraf and his officers were angry would be putting it mildly.

Later, the head of the U.S. Central Command was asked how close Pakistan and India had come to a nuclear war. He said, "Very. Both sides were on automatic pilot; both sides were escalating without much control. The danger of the situation was not fully appreciated. . . . I think one of the reasons that Musharraf and Nawaz Sharif were glad to see me come was that they had really scared themselves to death."

The Taliban in neighboring Afghanistan violently opposed the Kargil withdrawal. Although Taliban soldiers had been brought up and trained in Pakistan, Sharif had grown tired of the Taliban's radical ways. He asked them to shut down their terrorist training camps in Pakistan and warned them to stop sending terrorists into Pakistan. The stance was unusual, since Pakistan was one of only three countries that recognized the Taliban as the legitimate government in Afghanistan. Sharif even sent the chief of Pakistan's Inter-Services Intelligence to Kandahar, Afghanistan, to ask the one-eyed Taliban leader, Mullah Mohammed Omar, to control his Islamic militants, who were prowling in the Pakistani countryside.

It was never really known how much of the raid into Kargil was Musharraf's secret adventure or how much of it was known by the prime minister. Even so, the attack turned out to be an international political mess and a public snub of Pakistan by the United States.

Because of the tension from the Kargil incident, Sharif knew he had to get rid of Musharraf. He began a quiet campaign by creating tensions and misunderstandings between Musharraf and his staff. Sharif had used this method before to oust other government officials he no longer wanted. Little did Sharif know that he was setting Pakistan up for a coup that would remove his government from office.

Sharif even named Lieutenant General Khwaja Ziauddin to be Musharraf's successor and told officials in Washington. Politicians there approved of Sharif's new chief of army staff appointment.

Because of Sharif's incompetence, Musharraf was starting a campaign of his own. In mid-September, he called his army commanders together to discuss a move against the prime minister. Even though the generals agreed that Sharif's record was terrible, they decided there was no need to act unless there was a reason. One main reason would be if Sharif tried to replace yet another army commander. An

This photograph was taken just days after the coup that brought Musharraf to power in Pakistan. Musharraf (at rear, in center) declared himself the Pakistani chief executive and army chief, leading other nations to worry that a lengthy period of military rule was beginning.

advisor then warned Sharif not to take any actions against the army. If he were to do so, he could jeopardize his position. This warning went unheeded.

A Pakistani opponent to Sharif said, "The only thing that stood in the way of Sharif becoming a complete dictator was the army, and he was trying to manipulate the army to get his man on top."

There were also rumors that Sharif was treating the

Pakistani government as a family-run business and that he was showing contempt toward constitutional institutions. Sharif was rapidly spinning out of control. The army was the last institution that stood in his way to total control of Pakistan. Sharif's plan to take it over soon backfired, and he lost all he had worked to attain, the leadership of Pakistan.

6

The Coup

On October 12, 1999, General Pervez Musharraf led a coup against the democratically elected government of Pakistan. There had been rumors of the possibility of a coup, and Washington had even warned Sharif of it. In fact, the coup led by Musharraf was not an unusual occurrence in Pakistan, whose history is littered with coups and government takeovers.

In 1958, Iskandar Mirza, who had been president since 1956, instituted the first martial law in Pakistan and named General Ayub Khan as martial law administrator. The two could not get along, so Khan too over power from Mirza and declared himself president.

On March 25, 1969, General Khan gave up his power as the president after months of rioting. He handed his power over to General Yahya Khan.

On July 5, 1977, an elected prime minister, Zulfikar Ali Bhutto,

These members of the Pakistani army, seen in an October 15, 1999, photograph, are guarding the national Parliament building in the capital city of Islamabad. As part of the transfer of power from Sharif's government to the new military regime led by Pervez Musharraf, the army was dispatched to secure important sites.

was overthrown by a military coup led by General Zia-ul-Haq. It seemed as if for the Pakistani army, a coup was more a habit than a national disaster.

During the coup led by Musharraf, soldiers would not allow journalists into Prime Minister Sharif's house. The army also took over all government duties in the country. It shut down airports and allowed no planes to take off or land.

Sharif's staff remembered when the army came to get him: "In a flash, the army personnel were inside the prime minister's house as they checked all rooms and installed their automatic weapons at various places." Sharif became a prisoner in his own home.

Neighboring India was increasingly disturbed by the events unfolding. One senior Indian official said, "We are certainly not looking forward to a hardline army dictatorship in Islamabad."

Having Musharraf in power was a real concern because he was thought to have instigated the attack in Kargil. Also, because Sharif profited from trade with India, he was seen as easier to manipulate than Musharraf, who had no personal interests whatsoever in working with India.

India's fears were well founded. By November 1999, Musharraf rejected the Lahore Declaration and any agreements signed by Sharif. Indian government officials announced that they did not wish to interact with Musharraf. As time went by, India saw that this attitude was impractical and that Musharraf must be dealt with to manage the relationship between India and Pakistan.

President Clinton of the United States also watched the coup with concern. He said, "Pakistan's interests would be served by a prompt return to civilian rule and restoration of the democratic process."

On the night of the coup, a continuous strip moved across the bottom of the Pakistani TV screens. Pakistanis stayed close to their televisions and watched the strip that stated that Nawaz Sharif's government had been removed and that the chief of army staff would make an important announcement.

At 2:50 A.M., Musharraf appeared in his commando uniform and made the announcement to more than 140 million waiting Pakistanis: "I wish to inform you that the armed forces have moved in as a last resort to prevent any further destabilization. I have done so with all sincerity, loyalty and selfless devotion to the country with the armed forces firmly behind me." He urged his fellow countrymen to remain calm. He accused Sharif of completely demolishing institutions within the Pakistani government and causing the economy to collapse. Musharraf promised that in a short time he would announce what he planned to do for the future of Pakistan. He ended his speech with, "May Allah guide us on the path of truth and honor."

After Musharraf's broadcast, a party atmosphere took hold of the nation. Pakistanis seemed completely relieved that

Sharif's government had been ousted and the military had taken over. These actions showed just how unpopular Sharif's regime had become.

Forty-eight hours after the coup, Musharraf was posed with a perplexing issue. Musharraf's coup could be charged as high treason against the country. He appeared to be indecisive to the Pakistani public. Comments circulated that maybe the coup was a "spontaneous uprising." Experts on Pakistan stated, "Musharraf is a commando. He acted swiftly and decisively but did not think about what would happen next." A Western diplomat observing Pakistan's situation reported, "It doesn't look like they had an exit strategy worked out."

To settle this problem, the general took decisive action. He declared a state of emergency in Pakistan and put the constitution and National Assembly on hold. Musharraf's reasoning was to avoid having the National Assembly declare the coup unconstitutional. He was also concerned that it might vote against the military seizure of the country.

To avoid this, he sent troops to swarm over the Parliament building to prevent the National Assembly session. They ordered all staff members to leave the building. Then, the doors were slammed shut and locked. After appointing himself as the chief executive, Musharraf passed a law stating that his actions could not be challenged by any court of law.

Government workers were especially confused after the coup. They waited outside government buildings to return to work. Some approached gun-wielding soldiers to ask what was happening, only to be answered with silent stares. It seemed as if they were all wondering what was going to happen next.

Most Pakistanis were thrilled by Sharif's removal from power. They danced and waved flags in the streets. Sharif had almost driven Pakistan into a total collapse. Bribery was the norm, taxes were continuously avoided, and banks were lending huge amounts of money to politicians with no guarantee of being paid back.

In November 1999, less than a month after his bloodless coup, the new chief executive, Pervez Musharraf, held a press conference in which he outlined his plans for Pakistan to the international press corps.

In the meantime, Musharraf had refused to set a deadline for the return of democracy in Pakistan. He was quoted as saying to a news agency, "Whenever you give a time frame, a countdown starts and everyone gets into a standstill. The government machinery doesn't work seriously because they know that the time is limited and they start whiling away the time." One Pakistani journalist said, "The people here aren't really concerned with democracy anymore. They have seen what kind of democracy there is here. What we want is stability."

Because of this, it was agreed that martial law was the only way to run Pakistan until the other institutions were put back in place. A Pakistani politician felt that swift elections to restore democracy would be a mistake. He felt that it would take at least two years to get everything sorted out so democracy could be restored. Meanwhile, the pressure was on Musharraf to improve the common person's everyday existence. If this were not achieved, the general would soon find that his support from the people of Pakistan could turn into hostility.

A shiver of fear ran through the international community after the coup because of Pakistan's nuclear possibilities. But the United States was familiar with Musharraf and understood that he had had the power to press the nuclear button before the coup had taken place. Therefore, control of the weapons of mass destruction had not really switched hands. Even so, two of the three wars that had already taken place in South Asia in the past occurred while Pakistan was ruled by a military dictator like Musharraf.

After the coup, Great Britain stated that it had stopped assistance to the government of Pakistan. The British government had been spending about $33 million a year on Pakistani projects. It was reported that two-thirds of that money would be frozen because of the recent coup. Only money set aside for nongovernment projects would be released. The coup also caused other foreign investors and international lending programs, which Pakistan sorely needed, to have doubts.

Neighboring Iran also had concerns about the takeover. An Iranian news agency reported, "Pakistan, a country that has been ruled by unelected governments for 25 of its 52-year history, today opened another chapter of military rule. Prime

Minister Nawaz Sharif was dismissed by the man he had sacked, Army Chief General Pervez Musharraf."

The Saudi Arabian government gave Musharraf a nod of approval. Its defense secretary said, "We have great confidence in the Muslim armed forces of Pakistan and in their capacity to protect and serve Islam and all Pakistanis whoever they may be."

Asian nations cautiously expressed concern. China's foreign ministry stated, "Pakistan is China's friendly neighbor, and we are very concerned about changes there and are attempting to further comprehend the situation."

Musharraf was surprised by the mild international reaction to the coup of October 12. He was quite certain that within Pakistan he would be supported, saying: "I was pretty sure that the conditions were so bad that the people are going to accept change."

Even so, Prime Minister Nawaz Sharif refused to sign any papers indicating that he had resigned. Soon the stubborn Sharif found himself facing other troubles. He was charged with attempting to kill Musharraf by ordering the airport control tower not to allow his plane, which was low on fuel, to land. In addition, the military waged an all-out attack on Sharif. He was accused of plotting to dismantle the Pakistani army and of leaking military secrets. An investigation was looking into accusations of Sharif's misuse of his political power and of corruption during his time as prime minister.

Musharraf had to decide what to do with the fallen prime minister. He could not simply execute Sharif as General Zia-ul-Haq had done to Zulfikar Ali Bhutto in 1979. First, Sharif had many international contacts and friends. Second, Musharraf did not want to look like a military tyrant. He wanted to appear civil and democratic. The solution he chose was to exile Sharif to Saudi Arabia. Before this was done, however, Musharraf gallantly pardoned the ex–prime minister from his sentence of life in prison and forced him to pay $8.5 million to settle his corruption charges.

Musharraf did not find much opposition to his taking control of power. However, certain Islamic fundamentalists were not too happy about Musharraf's self-appointed position. This group was sometimes called the New Taliban. The Islamic radical groups wanted to enforce Muslim laws. They opposed Musharraf because of his slack approach to combining religion and politics.

Even though public opinion of Musharraf was high, the United States and the World Bank had their doubts about him. Musharraf had to somehow regain their trust in Pakistan and gain their trust in his ability to stand at the helm of the country.

Musharraf always had the assurance that the United States would not attack Pakistan or refuse it aid. Because of Pakistan's nuclear capabilities, the United States had an interest in keeping the nation stable. Politicians in Washington did discuss the possibility of increasing the sanctions against Pakistan. Instead of further penalizing the nation, some politicians felt that the relationship with Pakistan should be renewed.

Somehow, General Pervez Musharraf had taken control from a democratically elected prime minister. He had quieted any revolts against his position of power by ridding the country of Sharif and by putting the country under martial law. Now Musharraf needed to prove his effectiveness to his people. He needed to show that he could repair the failing economy and wipe out corruption in the highest ranks of the government. That was exactly what he set out to do.

7

General Musharraf Takes Control

Once firmly in power, Musharraf took little time to inform India how it would be treated. He said that if India showed Pakistan hostility, the same would be returned. If it issued threats, Pakistan would do the same. If India displayed peaceful intentions, though, Pakistan would also be willing to work for peace.

He was very adamant about settling the issue of Kashmir once and for all. He stated, "We would like to resolve all our differences, and when I say all our differences I mean the core issues of Kashmir first of all or simultaneously at least."

Even though India had its doubts about Musharraf, an Indian intelligence analyst said, "Pakistan would have become another Afghanistan—a territory without a state—had not the army moved in."

Because of Musharraf's extensive background in the Pakistani army, India regarded him as a soldier's general, not a general who

When he first took power in 1999, Musharraf (left) declared that the suspension of the constitution and regular elections would be temporary. After he assumed the presidency without election in June 2001, many observers questioned whether his continued leadership posed a threat to the eventual restoration of democracy in Pakistan.

appeased politicians. This fact gave India some assurance that when it did decide to talk with the new Pakistani leader, it would be talking to someone who had total control over the country.

After he was in power, Musharraf was interviewed by Mary Anne Weaver regarding Pakistan's views on Osama bin Laden and why he had been reluctant when he was chief of army staff to assist the United States in capturing him. In Mary Anne Weaver's book, *Pakistan: In the Shadow of Jihad and Afghanistan*, he said, "I've engaged with them endlessly about bin Laden, and I've told them that they must deal with him. . . . I've made it clear that it was in their interests to finally resolve it."

The real reason for Pakistan's reluctance was that the army could not support another war. The Pakistani army's resources were pushed to the limit with the continuous war in Kashmir.

Musharraf's political understanding impressed many people.

He did not dissolve the constitution and political assemblies but instead put them on hold. In addition, one of his speeches promised a bold move in Pakistan, granting equal rights to minorities.

Musharraf was trying to make the government of Pakistan secular, and he had problems with the many ethnic groups of the country. Because of Pakistan's diverse language and ethnic differences, unity was hard to establish. There were two different populations. Urban, or city, dwellers represented about 32 percent of the population, whereas rural, or country, inhabitants were about 68 percent. In these groups were a variety of landless peasants, herders, wealthy landowners, tribal leaders, and slum dwellers.

One of the largest problems that Musharraf faced was creating a united country. Within the country were several provinces and ethnic groups with governments of their own that were separated from the central government. A problem that no Pakistani government had ever addressed was how to include and accommodate the various ethnic groups in an overall federal system.

When Pakistan was first established, the hope was that the Islamic religion would create a bond strong enough to form a unified country. But this ideal had been proven wrong time and time again. Pakistan had no national identity. Pakistani citizens did not consider themselves Pakistani. Instead their urge was to help their ethnic group survive. This created a hostile environment without unified action toward a common goal and possibly accounted for the chaos within the country. Four main ethnic groups of differing sizes existed in Pakistan. The Punjabis made up about 57 percent of the population; the Pakhtuns, 13 percent; the Baluchis, 4 percent; and the Sindhis, 21 percent. Each group was trying to establish an identity that was unique.

Within these groups, it was traditional to exclude women from education. The level of their literacy was about 29 percent, and girls represented only a third of the school population. Because of strong Islamic groups in Pakistan, women must be subservient to men and are secluded.

Even though Musharraf wanted equal rights for minorities, he also made it clear that he wanted a distant relationship with the radical Islamic groups. He criticized the Islamic clergymen, and in one of his first major speeches, he said, "Islam teaches tolerance not hatred; universal brotherhood and not enmity; peace and not violence; progress and not bigotry."

To show he meant business, Musharraf pushed to change the blasphemy law. The law was established to ensure that people did not take the Prophet Muhammad's name in vain or treat the Koran without respect. The law allowed anyone to be accused of violating it without an investigation into the charges. The accused person was put in prison and given a death sentence. Musharraf wanted to modify the law so that an accused person received a proper investigation into the truthfulness of the accusation before imprisonment. But because of opposition, Musharraf's modifications were never put into effect.

Musharraf also wasted no time in executing his promises of taxing the rich and ridding Pakistan of corruption. A thorn in Musharraf's side was past rampant dishonesty among politicians and high army officials. His top priority was to revive the failing economy so he quickly established the National Accountability Bureau. Its purpose was to investigate and retrieve misappropriated funds. In turn, a list would be created of criminals who intentionally defaulted on their loans because of their political connections. All people accused would receive a speedy trial. This bureau earned much applause from the common citizen. Army officers looked over bank accounts, and suspicious ones were frozen. Several politicians were not allowed to leave the country, blocked from doing so at the international airport. One bank was reported to have written off $650 million in unpaid loans—a huge amount in comparison to the vast population of Pakistan living in complete poverty.

The former prime minister, Nawaz Sharif, was considered a prime suspect. In 1991, newspaper stories were released that stated that top politicians were putting pressure on banks to give them millions of dollars in loans. Nawaz Sharif was one of these politicians. In 1998, Sharif stated publicly that he would make his loans for millions of dollars current, which he never did. When Musharraf's military regime started accounting for all the money owed by politicians, the amount was $3 billion. Sharif had outstanding loans up to $50 million. Even with the vast amount of money that Sharif had funneled out of the country, he paid hardly any taxes. His tax statements from 1994 to 1996 indicated that he paid $10 in total. This was the type of corruption that Musharraf wanted to eliminate.

On the personal side, Musharraf was hard to fit in a specific category. He was considered a loving father and grandfather. He and his wife had two children, Ayla and Bilal, and one granddaughter, Ayla's child, Mariam. Musharraf also enjoyed sitting down to mentally stimulating entertainment and listening to music. He continued to love sports and the outdoors and got pleasure from playing squash, badminton, and golf. These pastimes were not usual for a commando soldier, especially one who had appointed himself the chief executive of a country.

Also unusual was the way Musharraf acted in public. The general had been accused of putting on a show while on television because of his dramatic behavior. He was also very conscientious about which outfit to wear for which audience. When meeting a Western diplomat, Musharraf could be found sporting three-piece Armani suits. If he had a meeting with Pakistani politicians, he wore his military uniform. Before speaking to the Pakistani public, Musharraf liked to put on his camouflage fatigues. Musharraf's observation of the splendid Turkish outfits when he was a young boy must have impressed him in his later years, making him realize that the right clothes could communicate the right message.

Even though Musharraf announced in 1999 that he regarded the Lahore Declaration as a farce, Pakistan and India had begun to establish groups to negotiate common-sense agreements on the use of nuclear weapons. The hope was that these groups would come up with terms that both countries could agree to and abide.

Musharraf addressed the Pakistan Institute of International Affairs on June 23, 2000. In his speech, he announced Pakistan's international policies. Several points that he brought up were: Pakistan should continue good relations with Iran, which would help stabilize Afghanistan; an all-out war with India should be avoided because of Indian nuclear capabilities, but Pakistan would continue to support the freedom fighters in Kashmir; terrorism and narcotics trafficking in Pakistan were condemned; and Pakistan wished to emerge as the leader of an Islamic bloc, or group of nations acting together for a common purpose.

Musharraf also continued to work on domestic policies. In May 2000, he promised that his government would take to trial people involved in honor killings. The victims of these types of killings were usually women thought to have betrayed or brought dishonor to their husbands or families. Husbands, family members, or fellow villagers carried out these killings. Musharraf said that honor killings would be treated the same as murder in a court of law.

In December 2000, Musharraf took the first steps to returning Pakistan to a democracy. He addressed the Pakistani people and announced that he could not have conquered Sharif's corrupt regime without some divine support. He restated that he would like democracy to return to Pakistan. He warned his people that they should nominate qualified and sincere representatives for coming elections. These would be candidates dedicated to public service. His last statement was that elections would soon take place for local self-governing bodies in Pakistan.

While working to establish democracy in his torn country, Musharraf slowly started to announce Pakistan's friendly policies in relation to India. On January 26, 2001, a severe earthquake shook the province of Gujarat in India. Bhuj, with more than 150,000 residents, was one of the largest cities in the

area. The entire city was turned to rubble, with very few buildings left standing. Basic services like water and electricity were
destroyed. Tens of thousands of people were killed or injured.
India was devastated by the loss.

Musharraf immediately reached out in friendship to his
neighbor by offering tents, medicine, and blankets. His gifts
were accepted and flown into India on Pakistan International
Airlines. Musharraf called Prime Minister Vajpayee of India
and expressed his deepest sympathy for the earthquake victims.
Vajpayee thanked Musharraf. These events marked the beginning of a thaw in relations between the two countries.

On May 24, 2001, Musharraf received an invitation from
Vajpayee to come to India in the summer for a summit meeting. Musharraf accepted and the summit was scheduled for July
14–16. It became known as the Agra Summit because it was
held in Agra, India.

Before the summit, India tried to show goodwill toward
Pakistan by making certain announcements: "It offered 20
scholarships to be awarded to Pakistani students to come and
study in India in subjects of their choice. . . . India announced
that it would not capture Pakistani fishermen who strayed into
its territorial waters. India also announced a decision to release
such Pakistani fishermen in Indian custody."

In response to India's concessions, Musharraf said that a
solution for Kashmir was the most important objective. When
pressed by Indian journalists about what type of solution was
needed, Musharraf said that he wanted the citizens of Kashmir
to vote and ultimately decide which country they would be
part of—India or Pakistan. This is how the United Nations
resolution of 1948 had stated the situation should be resolved.

Meanwhile, Musharraf was trying to handle problems within
Pakistan. He continued to attack Pakistan's extreme Islamic
leaders. He called them all to Islamabad in June 2001 to explain
his views on modernizing Islam. He asked, "How does the world
look at us? The world sees us as backward and constantly going

under. . . . It looks upon us as terrorists. We have been killing each other. And now we want to spread violence and terror abroad. . . . Our claim of tolerance is phony."

This speech represented a huge change in Pakistani politics. No leader of this Muslim country had dared to talk to the clerics in this manner. In addition, the new Pakistani leader did not hide the fact that he was not a strict Muslim.

On June 20, Musharraf declared to the world that he was the president of Pakistan, with no democratic election. Washington protested the move. But Musharraf felt it was important to establish himself as the legitimate leader of Pakistan before his arrival in India for the Agra Summit.

The first day of the summit, July 14, was filled with optimism even though hours before Musharraf's arrival, gunfire was exchanged between Pakistan and India along the Kashmir borders. A 21-gun salute welcomed Musharraf when he arrived in New Delhi, India. Musharraf visited the Mahatma Gandhi memorial. During British rule in India, Gandhi led the Indian people in passive-resistance demonstrations such as fasts and nationwide strikes to get the British to leave India. Musharraf was the first Pakistani leader to visit the memorial. He laid a wreath and showed respect for the peaceful Indian independence leader.

He also had the opportunity to revisit where he had been born in India. When he approached the haveli, he looked for a big gate that he remembered from his childhood but he could not find it. The people present expressed much warmth and love. He was impressed by the affection and was overheard saying, "Pray that the Lord improves the relations between India and Pakistan."

He was delighted to see a maid he had known so many years ago during his childhood. He grasped her hands and shook them, and then gave her an envelope with $200 in it. During their short stay in India, Musharraf and his wife won many hearts at the haveli with their kind behavior and acts.

Even though the first day of the summit was friendly, dis-agreements were starting to show between Musharraf and the

One of the most important policies Musharraf has undertaken since his rise to power has been the attempt to improve relations between Pakistan and India. In July 2001, Musharraf (left) held a summit with Indian Prime Minister Atal Behari Vajpayee (right). Although no major changes came from the talks, the summit was a significant step toward a thaw in the traditionally hostile relations between the two nations.

prime minister of India. Musharraf insisted on meeting with Kashmir separatist leaders. The leaders, who wanted Kashmir to be separated from India, promoted their cause by launching anti-India campaigns. The Indian government was furious that Musharraf would hold the meeting while visiting India and assigned one of its junior officials to attend as a representative.

The next day, a Sunday, Musharraf departed to have direct talks with Prime Minister Vajpayee. Nothing was settled, but they did agree to have a third round of talks the following day. During their discussions, heavy fighting continued between Indian soldiers and Islamic militants on the Kashmir borders, and 18 people were killed.

The last day of the Agra Summit was spent trying to find common ground so that the two leaders could sign a final statement. Nine hours and several draft proposals later, there was still no document that both leaders were willing to sign. The main problem was the issue of Kashmir. Finally, it was announced that no agreements could be made, and Musharraf returned to Pakistan.

On July 28, Vajpayee announced to the Indian National Executive, "General Musharraf came to Agra as a military man with a specific self-serving goal and was not serious about restoring peace. An inescapable conclusion to be drawn is that there is not even a tentative meeting ground on the substance of political issues at discussion between India and Pakistan."

Even though these harsh words were spoken and there was bitter disappointment on both sides, there had been some success in the talks. Pakistan and India agreed to have further meetings. In addition, Vajpayee had been invited to visit Islamabad later in the year.

Musharraf was trying to prove to the world that he was the legitimate leader of Pakistan. It was not until the events of September 11, 2001, however, that this leader would receive international attention and praise.

8

Pakistan and September 11, 2001

After terrorists attacked the World Trade Center in New York City and the Pentagon in Washington, D.C., on September 11, 2001, officials from the United States confronted Pervez Musharraf. Because Pakistan's connection with the Taliban in Afghanistan was well known in the international community, Musharraf was given an ultimatum. He would have to choose whether to continue his support of the Taliban or to assist the United States in its war against the terrorists in Afghanistan. Musharraf was told, "You are either 100 percent with us or 100 percent against us. There is no gray area."

The choice was very difficult for Musharraf, since his country was filled with Islamic extremists who supported the Taliban and Osama bin Laden. He also was reluctant to abandon the Taliban, as he had always given support to its leader, Mullah Mohammed Omar.

After radical Muslim terrorists attacked the United States on September 11, 2001, U.S. President George W. Bush (right) requested the assistance of Pakistan in the effort to remove the government of Afghanistan and eliminate terrorists. Although many of his people disagreed with his decision, Musharraf (left) promised to help the United States in its war against terrorism.

The reasons for this support were complex and had nothing to do with Musharraf admiring or agreeing with the strict religious practices of the Taliban. Because the Taliban had been created in Pakistan, its leadership was sensitive to Pakistan and its issues. These close ties guaranteed peace between Pakistan and Afghanistan. This allowed Pakistan to concentrate on its prime enemy, India.

Even so, Musharraf realized that the United States had no intention of allowing the Taliban government to continue.

With this in mind, he made a very quick decision. He immediately informed Washington that Pakistan would fully cooperate with the United States in its war against terror.

Musharraf's government was then told what it needed to provide to the United States: Pakistan must not allow Al Qaeda members to cross the borders into Pakistan. This would include stopping any arms going from Pakistan into Afghanistan. The United States must be given all over-flight and landing rights for its aircraft and full access to Pakistan's naval bases, airbases, and borders. In addition, Pakistan needed to provide the United States with intelligence support. Musharraf must then announce that he and the people of Pakistan condemned the terrorist attacks of September 11. He also had to make a plan to cut back on terrorism within Pakistan. In addition, the government of Pakistan must stop all fuel supplies and all supporters of the Taliban within Pakistan from entering Afghanistan.

Musharraf asked for certain things in return for his support. He asked the United States to lift the sanctions against his country that had been put into place because of past nuclear testing. He also requested financial aid from the United States to assist the Pakistani economy. Musharraf advised the United States to make clear that the terrorism campaign was not one against Islam but against specific terrorist acts. These conditions were acceptable to the United States and were granted to Musharraf.

Musharraf made it clear that the United States could use Pakistan as an operational and logistical facility. However, the Pakistani army would not be involved in any operations in Afghanistan against Osama bin Laden and the Taliban. Musharraf told the United States that Pakistan did not agree with the removal of the Taliban in Afghanistan. "It was only after the failure of negotiations between the Pakistani government delegation and the delegation of religious leaders of Pakistan with the Taliban that Musharraf changed this approach."

Before Musharraf announced the agreements made with the United States to the people of Pakistan, he had to get the consent of his army commanders. He gathered them together and argued his points for up to six hours. He said that if Pakistan did not cooperate, it would be labeled a terrorist country. He also pointed out that India would use Pakistan's noncooperation against it, allowing the Indian government to obtain favors from the United States. Another concern Musharraf had was that the United States would destroy Pakistan's nuclear and missile facilities if it did not cooperate. Lastly, because of sanctions, Pakistan's government was severely short of income and its military supplies and equipment were running dangerously low. Musharraf claimed that if Pakistan assisted the United States, the sanctions would be lifted and financial aid would be given.

Even after hearing all of the issues, some commanders were less than excited about Musharraf's cooperation with the United States. One lieutenant general said, "Musharraf's policies are wrong, and they do not serve the long-term interests of Pakistan."

In a speech to the Pakistani people on September 19, 2001, Musharraf sounded like he was apologizing. He felt he had no other choice and explained to his people that America had three targets: Osama bin Laden, the Taliban, and an international war on terror. He then listed the demands that the United States had made on Pakistan. To help his audience comprehend the important nature of the situation, he said, "We in Pakistan are facing a very critical situation. . . . If we make the wrong decisions, our vital interests will be harmed. . . . It's not a question of bravery or cowardice. But bravery without thinking is stupidity." He went on to defend the decision regardless of what the Islamic extremists wanted. He said, "How do we best serve Afghanistan's interests? By going against the world community or by working with the international community. I am sure you will agree with me that we can only do the latter." He ended this monumental speech with, "I ask you to trust me, like you trusted me when I went to Agra. May Allah guide and protect us."

Musharraf displayed amazing bravery with his speech. "He believed Pakistan's very survival was at stake. . . . He abandoned his government's sponsorship of the Taliban and confronted tens of thousands of angry demonstrators on his streets, whose loyalties were not so much with him as they were with Osama bin Laden, Pakistan militant Islamists, and the Taliban."

Several of these protesters were men, born in poor, landless families, who were handed over to the madrasas at a very early age. At these schools, they memorized the Koran and prayed. They were taught to believe that America and Israel want to destroy all Muslims and that Islam was a religion that would take over the world.

After the U.S. bombing started in Afghanistan in October 2001, many Western journalists were in Pakistan to record the events. They videotaped images of bearded men yelling furiously while burning crude handmade likenesses of President Bush and General Musharraf. There were international concerns that a civil war could break out in Pakistan.

Despite these fears, fewer and fewer people protested against Musharraf. The leader saw that the majority of the Pakistani people were on his side. However, Musharraf still had to take extreme measures against radical Muslim groups. He arrested the leaders of Jamaat-e-Islami, a fundamental Islamic group in Pakistan. The accounts of militant Islamic groups in Pakistan that were on the U.S. list of international terrorist organizations were frozen. Resentment became widespread against Musharraf, and he became concerned about opposition from officials high in his own army. He quickly retired or transferred seven of his eleven senior military contemporaries because they opposed his continued support of the United States and the actions he was taking within Pakistan against extreme Islamic groups.

In places, the people of Pakistan rose in violent rebellion against Musharraf's support for the United States. Here, a religious student is burning an effigy of President George W. Bush in October 2001. The protesters chanted slogans against both the United States and President Musharraf.

Musharraf found himself doing a juggling act. On one hand, he had to appease the U.S. government, and on the other hand, he had to maintain his position in Pakistan as a strong leader and not completely alienate the Pakistani people.

Pakistan's close ties to the Taliban did not help matters. Since the 1990s, the Pakistani military had supported the Taliban because it supplied fresh soldiers to fight in Kashmir. After September 11, the United States would no longer turn a blind eye to the Taliban-Pakistan connection.

On October 30, 2001, two prominent Pakistani nuclear scientists were arrested, charged with having ties to the Taliban

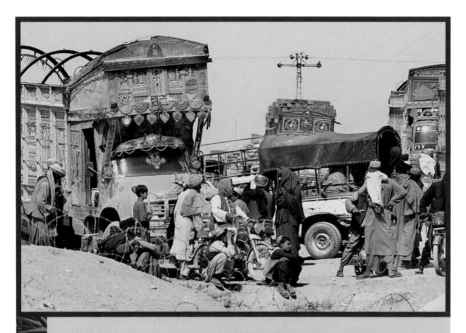

As part of the war against terrorism, Pakistan closed its border to Afghanistan, to help prevent terrorists or Taliban leaders from escaping. Here, Afghan refugees are seen waiting for the borders to reopen.

regime. The international worry was that these two scientists might have been helping Osama bin Laden develop nuclear weapons. Bin Laden had stated in the past that he felt it was his religious duty to pursue and acquire such weapons. These two men were later released.

In November 2001, Musharraf finally admitted to the United States that his government had used Taliban soldiers in the fight for Kashmir. The United States again ordered him to cut ties to the Taliban.

When the bombing began in Afghanistan, many of the Taliban chose not to fight. Instead, they packed their things and moved back home to Pakistan. Although they were probably relieved to be alive, they began to resent the harsh betrayal shown by government leaders in Islamabad. Once these ex-Taliban soldiers returned to Pakistan, they were eager to link up with other radical Islamic groups.

Musharraf ordered Pakistani security forces to become border patrols between Pakistan and Afghanistan because he wanted to keep Taliban soldiers, as well as Afghan refugees, out of Pakistan. Musharraf knew that it would be difficult for Pakistan to support destitute refugees financially and that they would become a huge burden on Pakistan's failing economy. Musharraf also did not want Taliban soldiers moving into the northern part of Pakistan disguised as refugees. In addition, Musharraf closed down terrorist camps in Pakistan.

Even after these efforts, Islamic militants within Pakistan planned and executed actions that went unchecked. On October 1, 2001, terrorists stormed the heavily guarded Jammu and Kashmir State Assembly while it was in session. Firing automatic weapons, they killed five policemen, a schoolgirl, and six assembly employees. A suicide bomber drove a jeep filled with explosives up to the main entrance. The jeep blew up into a huge ball of fire. In the end, 40 people died. A Pakistani militant group claimed it was responsible for the attack.

The final straw came on December 13, 2001, when five men armed with rifles, grenades, and other explosives drove toward the Parliament in India. They were not stopped, since their car looked legitimate. It was painted with official markings and had a red light on the roof. Once the car arrived in front of the Parliament, the five men jumped out and began firing. After 30 minutes, six Indian security guards and one gardener had been killed. No one claimed to have any idea who was behind this assault.

The response from Washington was varied. The terrorist attack was condemned, and bank accounts of the suspected terrorist groups were frozen. President Bush called Prime Minister Vajpayee and expressed his deepest sympathy. On the other hand, the Indian government was advised to be careful in its reaction and to hold back on retaliation. The White House did not want Pakistan distracted in any way from the war in Afghanistan.

Nevertheless, India immediately blamed Pakistani Islamic militants and responded by cutting rail links to Pakistan. Musharraf denied having anything to do with the attack and challenged the Indian government to come up with hard evidence of Pakistan's involvement. India continued defensive actions and moved missiles, fighter planes, and thousands of troops to the border of Pakistan. Rumors of possible nuclear war were beginning to circulate. Musharraf realized that he had to issue a major crackdown. "On 12 January, 2002 he delivered a landmark speech in which he announced a ban of two of the most prominent Pakistan-based militant groups." He also froze the group's assets and arrested 2,000 Islamic extremists. The reasons he gave were to show support for the U.S.-led war on terror and to stabilize the escalating situation between Pakistan and India. Even though relations remained tense, India backed down.

In the same speech, Musharraf announced that Pakistan's position in Kashmir had not changed and that there would be no compromise. He said, "Kashmir remains a part of the bloodstream of Pakistanis."

Musharraf's attack on the Pakistani militant groups antagonized them and on January 23, 2002, Daniel Pearl, a journalist with the *Wall Street Journal*, was kidnapped in Karachi. Pearl had arranged an interview with a radical Muslim group with ties to Al Qaeda. He was working on a story about Richard Reid, a man arrested in December after he tried to ignite his explosive shoes on a plane headed to Miami.

Pearl was led to believe that the group had information about Reid. Four days after Pearl's arranged interview, an e-mail message was received by Pakistani and international media. It stated that the journalist had been kidnapped and it showed a picture of Pearl with a gun pointed at his head. A second e-mail message demanded that the United States send back all captured Pakistanis from the war in Afghanistan. The captured men were being held on a U.S. naval base in Guantanamo Bay, Cuba. In the second e-mail, the kidnappers threatened to kill Pearl if their demands were not met within 24 hours.

The U.S. and Pakistani governments began to search extensively for the missing journalist. Ahmad Omar Saeed Sheikh, a British-educated militant, was soon arrested, but there was no clear idea as to Pearl's whereabouts. On February 22, 2002, the world found out through gruesome videotaped images that Daniel Pearl had been stabbed to death.

Musharraf tried to explain the senseless crime. He felt that Islamic extremists had committed it to destabilize the government in Pakistan. It was their way of getting back at Musharraf for issuing a crackdown on Islamic militants. If Musharraf's fears were well founded, then there was international concern that more acts of terror would be committed within Pakistan against Americans and Western journalists. Another concern was that the groups would continue their despicable acts until Musharraf backed down on supporting the United States and trying to get rid of Al Qaeda and the Taliban.

Even with all the turmoil, Pakistan soon reaped its reward for supporting the United States on the Taliban issue. The country received $3 billion in aid. In addition, Musharraf managed to change his international image. Before September 11, he had been thought of as a military dictator who needed to restore democracy in Pakistan. Because of his decision to cooperate with the United States, though, his survival as the leader of Pakistan became very important to the Western world. Even though he used controversial methods to become the leader of Pakistan, his good judgment and firm leadership began to put Pakistan on the road of advancement. However, the issue of Kashmir still needed to be addressed, an issue very close to Musharraf's heart.

9

The Future of President Musharraf and Pakistan

The battle between Pakistan and India over the Kashmir area continues today. They volley missiles at each other from a harsh area, 20,000 feet (6,096 meters) high, called Siachen Glacier. This area has the greatest concentration of high peaks in the world. The Siachen Glacier's melting water provides a constant flow to the river Indus. This river's lifegiving water is extremely important to Pakistan and India. The icy, barren region is definitely misnamed since *Siachen* means "the place of roses." The area received the name because flowers once bloomed in the valleys way below the frigid peaks. The continuous battle in the harsh environment of Siachen Glacier costs Pakistan $6,000 per

These Indian soldiers are on patrol along the Line of Control that divides the disputed area of Kashmir. By 2000, when this photograph was taken, India and Pakistan had already fought two wars over Kashmir and were preparing for a third.

soldier per year. Eighty percent of the casualties from this war are not from wounds. Soldiers die because of the extremely cold surroundings.

It became evident to India and the United States that the Pakistani army still used former Taliban and Al Qaeda soldiers for support in the fight for Kashmir. The battle for the region had become an ongoing jihad. Because of Pakistan's cooperation with the United States in the war against terror, the White House had become much more lenient toward Pakistan's activities in Kashmir. Pakistan's continued warfare was no longer labeled a terrorist action as it had been in the past. Officials in Washington had even asked the government of India to not seek disciplinary actions against Pakistani terrorists in Kashmir.

It seemed to the Indian politicians that Washington displayed favoritism toward Pakistan. There was concern that the United States was no longer interested in the Kashmir issue and that Pakistan was receiving military support from the White House. The United States reassured India that its relationship with Pakistan in no way hindered or diminished the long-term relationship Washington has had with the Indian government.

Even so, in early 2002, representatives of the United States, Britain, Russia, and China met India's prime minister. The purpose was to discuss Pakistan. The prime minister was advised to react with moderation and restraint because Pakistan had recently taken several steps to rid itself of terrorist organizations and religious extremists. The four representatives explained that if Pakistan was pressured too hard by India, it might withdraw its previous positive actions against terrorism. They also stated that India and Pakistan needed to take major steps to resolve the Kashmir problem because of their nuclear capabilities.

It was also suggested that because of Pakistan and India's combined efforts on the international war on terror, a common ground could be found to open the door to constructive dialogue between the two nations. This might finally bring peace along the borders of Pakistan and India.

Officials in the United States have tried to help India and Pakistan come to a resolution over the Kashmir area. Even so, it was understood that Osama bin Laden's soldiers, or other Pakistani Islamic militants who do not take orders from the army of Pakistan, could easily sabotage any resolution.

Because of his alliance with the United States, Musharraf feared that the soldiers who had been trained in Pakistan's madrasas would now turn on him. Some of these fears were realized on May 14, 2002, when three men entered an Indian

Pervez Musharraf often uses his public appearances to appeal to different parts of Pakistani and international society. Sometimes those efforts have been unsuccessful. For example, when Musharraf posed for this photograph with his pet dogs, he offended many radical Muslims, who consider dogs impure.

army camp and cruelly killed 34 people, most of whom were women and children. On June 14, a car bomb blew up outside the United States consulate in Karachi, killing 12 and injuring 50 people. Then, on Christmas Day, terrorists walked into a Catholic church in a small Christian town in Pakistan called Daska and threw a grenade during the service. After the smoke cleared, three people had been killed and eight wounded.

The gap between Musharraf and the Islamic extremists continued to grow wider. He further aggravated the *mullahs*, or Muslim teachers, by appearing in photographs with his two pet dogs. This was an insult to radical Muslims, who consider dogs impure.

Pervez Musharraf is sometimes described as a chameleon.

He is a man who can do almost anything he sets his mind to. Since he has control over more than 146 million people in the Muslim world and 30 to 50 nuclear bombs, the hope is that the chameleon aspect of his personality will turn out to favor peace, not war. The world also hopes that he will be strong enough to reform Pakistan's economy and soothe religious differences. If he fails, fanatical Islamic soldiers could take over and Muslim clergy could rule the country, like in Iran. Another possibility might be absolute chaos, and in the middle of the disorder, a switch to fire several atomic bombs.

Today, Islamic fundamentalists brag that in ten years they will have complete control of the Pakistani army. This conjures up a deadly image for the rest of the world. A fanatical religious group would then have its finger on the trigger of an atomic bomb. The United States, India, and China are unsure what to do about this possibility.

Fear of a similar situation began after the coup led by Musharraf, with concerns that the new leadership could irresponsibly release a nuclear bomb. But it was soon realized that even though Pakistan has had democratically elected governments throughout the years, "control over Pakistan's [nuclear] capability has always remained with the military." So, in fact, the control of the bomb never actually changed hands.

Another international concern is that Pakistan will begin making bombs that could be sold to other Muslim countries, such as Libya or Saudi Arabia. Some Indian officials have expressed concern about a religious union formed by Muslim countries. This could make a nuclear bomb available to the whole union, thus creating an Islamic bomb held by a group that is not controlled by a nation with which to negotiate.

Pakistan has denied such claims. In 1999, however, Saudi Arabia did show interest in Pakistan's nuclear program. The Saudi crown prince and his defense secretary visited Pakistan's nuclear plant. In May 2000, the minister of information for

In January 2003, Pakistani military scientists formally presented the new Ghauri missile (seen here) to President Musharraf near the city of Islamabad.

Saudi Arabia's neighbor, the United Arab Emirates, also visited one of Pakistan's plants. The minister spoke to Khan and asked him for help in creating a bomb. Khan said that he could train personnel in the United Arab Emirates.

There has been strong evidence that when President Bill Clinton was in office, Pakistan's top nuclear weapons scientists were helping North Korea. Instead of selling nuclear technology, Pakistan exchanged it for long-range missiles. The missiles would allow Pakistan to launch nuclear bombs deep within India if needed. Pakistan has denied these charges.

A senior Clinton administration official remarked on this exchange: "Our concerns were addressed to the Pakistanis at the highest levels. . . . Our concern was about whether the

Pakistani government was sufficiently in control of its nuclear labs and certain nuclear scientists."

There is no evidence today that Pakistan has sold its nuclear secrets. Instead Pakistan has remained one of the eight nuclear powers in the world. Those nuclear powers are the United States, Russia, China, Britain, France, India, Israel, and Pakistan. However, Pakistan's national debt is nearly $40 billion, which, along with its ever-expanding population, leads Pakistan to constantly seek foreign currency. Pakistani officials could easily be tempted to sell their valuable nuclear secrets to unauthorized countries to bolster the sagging economy.

There was also concern as to how many bombs Pakistan intends to make. Today, Musharraf has confirmed that Pakistan does not plan to make enough to match India's arsenal. It was commonly known that Islamabad does not have the financial ability to do this, but it was rumored that Pakistan had a larger nuclear bomb arsenal than India has. A U.S. general said, "Don't assume that the Pakistani capability is inferior to the Indians. India . . . has no nuclear-capable missiles and fewer aircrafts capable of delivering a nuclear payload than Pakistan does."

Musharraf has managed to change the world's perception of him. First thought of as an unlawful military dictator bent on making war with India, he is now seen as a reasonable, moderate leader who is dedicated to the war on terror and who also wants peace with his Indian neighbor.

Politically, Musharraf has to balance on a very fine line. Even though he has taken many efforts to distance himself from hard-line Islamic terrorist groups, he will not be able to completely sever his connections. His survival as the president of Pakistan relies on not pushing these groups to the point where they will attack him.

Those close to President Musharraf observe that he has many personality characteristics. He is known to work steadily toward his goals. Even so, he does not make his goals alone. On important decisions, he consults others. Musharraf is an excellent listener and encourages those under him to speak their minds freely. He returns loyalty with loyalty to those close to him. Within Pakistan, freedom of speech has not been completely taken away. Instead of suppressing criticism of him, he is known to allow the media to let off steam. One area he is faulted for is his ability to analyze situations and make good judgments. His behavior can appear impulsive. Because of his commando army training, Musharraf has a tendency to use rough language and can appear to act brave and steadfast but always ready to use any method to get what he wants.

In April 2002, Musharraf took a bizarre route to restoring democracy. He announced a nationwide referendum. The purpose of the referendum was a five-year extension to his office of presidency. If people voted for Musharraf, it indicated that they endorsed his policies and a new five-year term. Before the referendum, Musharraf went on a month-long campaign to promote himself. During this time, he banned any public rallies against the referendum.

Seven days before the referendum, nine judges were reviewing four petitions brought before them by groups that opposed it. These groups felt that the referendum was unconstitutional and went directly against an earlier Supreme Court ruling that Musharraf was to hand over his power to an elected government in October.

Musharraf adamantly denied there was any wrongdoing. He argued that the referendum was not unconstitutional because referendums can be held on important matters. However, the constitution of Pakistan stated that national and state assemblies and the senate must elect the leader of Pakistan.

The referendum took place on April 30, 2002, and 97.5 percent of the vote was in favor of Musharraf. However, there was evidence of dishonest dealings and forcing people to vote.

Pakistan's Supreme Court ordered Musharraf, the self-appointed president, to hold democratic elections by October 2002. On October 10, 2002, Musharraf fulfilled his commitment

Although Pervez Musharraf has made great strides toward changing the government of Pakistan and improving his country's relationships with the rest of the world, it remains to be seen whether he can ultimately bring peace to his troubled nation.

to democracy by holding the elections. The purpose of the elections was to vote for the national parliament and four provincial legislatures. Almost 100 political parties participated. The elections turned violent with shootouts between the political rivals; six people were killed.

During the election, a new prime minister was elected, and on November 23, 2002, Musharraf swore Prime Minister Mir Zafarullah Khan Jamali into office. Musharraf transferred his powers as chief executive over to the newly elected cabinet.

A daunting issue Musharraf continues to face today is Kashmir. On February 5, 2003, Musharraf made a speech accusing India of supporting terrorism in Kashmir. He called upon India to make peace with Pakistan and to stop domination in Kashmir. He asked again for the referendum ordered by the United Nations resolution of 1948 to allow the people of Kashmir and Jammu to vote on which country to join. To date, this problem remains unresolved.

With Pakistan's internal problems, continual battles with India over Kashmir and Jammu, military takeovers, and non-democratic ways, some Pakistanis have begun to doubt the wisdom of establishing Pakistan in the first place. Some wonder what the founder of Pakistan, Muhammad Ali Jinnah, was thinking more than 50 years ago at the inception of Pakistan. One Pakistani author, Mohammed Anwar Khan, wrote, "The Pakistani system is neither Islamic nor democratic. Then what did Jinnah create fifty years ago?" The hope for all Pakistanis is that President Pervez Musharraf, with the help of the newly elected prime minister, will finally bring Pakistan into an era where peace and prosperity will reign.

1943	**August 11** Born in Delhi before India gained independence from Great Britain.
1947	Moved to Karachi, Pakistan, during the Partition.
1949–1957	Musharraf's father was transferred to Ankara, Turkey, to work at the Pakistani Embassy. Musharraf spent his early childhood there.
1957	Moved to Karachi. He attended St. Patrick's High School and Forman Christian College in Lahore.
1961–1964	Musharraf joined the Pakistan Military Academy, located at Kakul.
1965	Decorated with a medal called Mention in the Dispatches during the 1965 Indo-Pakistan War.
1968	**December 28** Married Begum Sehba.
1971–1973	Served as a major and fought in the war against East Pakistan.
1973–1979	Musharraf attended the Command and Staff College in Quetta and the National Defense College. After his education, he was promoted to lieutenant colonel.
1979–1985	Musharraf became involved in helping prepare the fighters called the mujaheddin in a war against the Soviet Union in Afghanistan.
1985–1987	Musharraf was encouraged by General Zia-ul-Haq to put together a Special Snow Warfare Force. With the new force, Musharraf launched an attack on an Indian post at Bilafond Pass in the Kashmir area.
1988	**May** General Musharraf, with the help of Osama bin Laden's Al Qaeda fighters, suppressed an uprising by the Shiites in Gilgit, Pakistan.
1989–1990	Musharraf commanded an artillery unit. He also served as a deputy military secretary and a member of the War Wing of the National Defense College.
1991	Was promoted to major general.
1993–1995	Served as director general of military operations at the General Headquarters.
1998	Nuclear testing began in Pakistan, and General Musharraf was appointed chief of army staff.
1999	Seized power in a bloodless coup on October 12. Took the role of chief executive of Pakistan.

2001   **June 20** Appointed himself president of Pakistan.

July 14 Arrived in New Delhi for talks with Indian Prime Minister Shri Atal Behari Vajpayee. Talks ended in failure two days later.

September 11 United States gave Musharraf an ultimatum regarding the war against terrorism. Musharraf decided to side with the United States.

December 13 Pakistan blamed for suicide attack on Indian Parliament.

2002   **January 12** Musharraf declared crackdown on religious extremism and banned two of the most prominent Pakistan-based militant groups.

April Pakistan set referendum on April 30 to vote on whether Musharraf would remain as president for another five years. He received overwhelming support.

October 10 Musharraf fulfilled his commitment to democracy by holding elections for the Parliament and four provincial legislatures.

November 23 President Musharraf swore Prime Minister Mir Zafarullah Khan Jamali into office. Musharraf transferred his powers as chief executive over to the newly elected cabinet.

2003   **February 5** Musharraf made a speech again urging India to support a referendum to determine the status of Kashmir.

FURTHER READING

Ali, Tariq. *The Clash of Fundamentalisms: Crusades, Jihads and Modernity.* London and New York: Verso, 2002.

Caldwell, John C. *Major World Nations, Pakistan.* Philadelphia: Chelsea House Publishers, 2000, 2001.

Deady, Kathleen W. *Countries of the World, Pakistan.* Mankato, MN: Bridgestone Books, 2001.

Dixit, J.N. *India-Pakistan in War and Peace.* New Delhi: Books Today, 2002.

Jones, Owen Bennett. *Pakistan: Eye of the Storm.* New Haven and London: Yale University Press, 2002.

Mohan, Major Sulakshan. *Pakistan Under Musharraf.* Delhi: Indian Publishers Distributors, 2000.

Weaver, Mary Anne. *Pakistan: In the Shadow of Jihad and Afghanistan.* New York: Farrar, Straus and Giroux, 2002.

Weiss, Anita M., and S. Zulfiqar Gilani, eds., *Power and Civil Society in Pakistan.* Oxford: Oxford University Press, 2001.

Harrison, Selig, 33
haveli, Musharraf's early years in,
16-17, 75
Hindus
beliefs of, 17-18
and conflict with Muslims at
independence, 17-20
and Kashmir, 21-23
honor killings, 73

India
and Agra Summit, 74, 75, 77, 82
and Bhutto, 30
and British rule, 17
and earthquake in Gujarat, 73-74
and independence, 17
and Indo-Pakistan War, 28
and Kargil incident, 38, 48, 49, 53,
55-57
and Lahore Declaration, 52-53, 62, 72
and Musharraf as chief of army
staff, 52
Musharraf born in, 16-17, 75
and Musharraf handling relations
with Pakistan and, 62, 68-69,
72-74, 75, 77, 79, 81
and Musharraf's coup, 61-62
and Musharraf siding with United
States after September 11, 2001, 81
and nuclear weapons, 38, 42-43,
44, 48, 56, 72-73, 90, 92, 94
Pakistan acquiring long-range
missiles against, 93
and Partition, 18-20
and religious strife at independence,
17-20
and terrorist attack on Parliament,
85-86
and United States, 90
and Vajpayee, 52-53, 74, 77, 85
See also Kashmir
Indo-Pakistan War, 28
Inter-Services Intelligence
and Musharraf's coup, 14
and Taliban, 39, 57

Iran
and Khomeini, 30-31
and madrasas, 33
and Musharraf's coup, 65-66
and Pakistan, 73
Islamic extremists, and Musharraf,
24, 34, 67, 71, 74-75, 78-87, 90-91,
92, 94
See also Taliban
Israel, and madrasas, 82

Jamaat-e-Islami, 82
Jamali, Mir Zafarullah Khan, 96, 97
Jammu
and origin of dispute between
India and Pakistan, 21-23
and United Nations, 23, 97
See also Kashmir
jihad, 33
Jinnah, Muhammad Ali, 97

Karachi, Musharraf restoring order
in, 52
Karamat, Jehangir, 39
Kargil incident, 38, 48, 49, 53, 55-57,
62
Kashmir
and Bilafond Pass, 34-35
and Instrument of Accession,
22-23
and Kargil incident, 38, 48, 49,
53, 55-57, 62
and Lahore Declaration, 62
and Line of Control, 21-22, 53
and mujaheddin, 38-39
and Musharraf, 12, 23, 29, 34-35,
38, 53, 55-57, 62, 69, 73-74,
75, 77, 83, 84, 86, 87, 88-90,
96-97, 99
and origin of dispute between
India and Pakistan, 21-23
and Pakistan's army resources,
69
and Shamir, 12
and Siachen Glacier, 88-89

and Yahya Khan, 60
and Lahore Declaration, 52-53, 62,
   72
and madrasas, 33-34, 39, 82
Muslims in, 19-20, 23
and nuclear weapons, 38, 41, 42-46,
   48-49, 56, 65, 67, 72-73, 81, 90,
   92-94
and religious strife at formation of,
   17-20
and sanctions, 45, 46, 48, 81
and Sharif, 39-41, 46, 48, 49, 50-53,
   55-59, 60-67
and Soviet invasion of Afghanistan,
   31, 33-34, 38, 45-46, 48
and support of Taliban, 39, 57
and support of United States
   against Taliban, 78-87
terrorist training camps in, 33, 52,
   57
and Zia-ul-Haq, 30, 32-33, 34, 38,
   60, 66
See also Kashmir; Musharraf,
   Pervez
Pakistan Institute of International
   Affairs, 73
Pakistan Military Academy, 25, 26-28
Pakistan People's Party, 30
Partition, 18-20
Pearl, Daniel, 86-87
Project 706, 44

Reid, Richard, 86
Royal College of Defense Studies, 38

St. Patrick's High School, 24
Saudi Arabia
   as Middle Eastern power, 31
   and Musharraf's coup, 66
   and Pakistan's nuclear program,
      92
   Sharif exiled in, 66
Sehba, Begum (wife), 28, 72, 75
September 11, 2001, Pakistan's support
   of United States after, 78-87

Sharif, Nawaz
   and army capabilities, 41
   and corruption, 71-72
   and declaration of emergency and
      suspension of rights, 46
   and incompetence, 57-59
   and Kargil incident, 48, 55-57
   and Lahore Declaration, 52-53, 62,
      72
   and Musharraf as chief of army
      staff, 49, 50-52, 55-57
   and Musharraf's coup, 12-16, 57-
      59, 60-67
   and nuclear weapons, 41, 46, 48,
      53
   as prime minister, 39-41
   and Taliban, 57
Sheikh, Ahmad Omar Saeed, 87
Shiites, revolt of, 36-38
Sikhs
   beliefs of, 18
   and conflict with Muslims at
      independence, 17-20
Soviet Union, and invasion of
   Afghanistan, 31, 33-34, 38, 45-46
Special Services Group (SSG), 28-30
Special Snow Warfare Force, 34-35
Sunnis, 36
Sweden, and Pakistan's nuclear
   weapons, 45
Syed line, 17

Taliban
   and jihad, 33
   and Kargil withdrawal, 56-57
   and Kashmir, 83, 84, 89, 90
   and madrasas, 33-34, 39
   Musharraf ending support of after
      September 11, 2001, 78-87
   Musharraf monitoring conduct of
      in Afghanistan, 39
   Musharraf supporting, 33-34, 39, 57
   and return to Pakistan from
      Afghanistan, 84-85
   and Sharif, 57

page:

2:    AFP/NMI
11:   21st Century Publishing
13:   Reuters Photo Archive/NMI
16:   Reuters Photo Archive/NMI
19:   AP/Wide World Photos
22:   KRT/NMI
27:   Reuters Photo Archive/NMI
31:   Zuma Press/NMI
32:   AP/Wide World Photos
37:   Reuters Photo Archive/NMI
40:   Reuters Photo Archive/NMI
43:   Hulton Getty Photo Archive/NMI
47:   © AFP/CORBIS
51:   Reuters Photo Archive/NMI

54:   Reuters Photo Archive/NMI
58:   Reuters Photo Archive/NMI
61:   Reuters Photo Archive/NMI
64:   Reuters Photo Archive/NMI
69:   AFP/NMI
76:   AFP/NMI
79:   KRT/NMI
83:   AFP/NMI
84:   AFP/NMI
89:   KRT/NMI
91:   KRT/NMI
93:   AFP/NMI
96:   AFP/NMI

Cover: Reuters Photo Archive/NMI
Frontis: AFP/NMI

SARA LOUISE KRAS has had several nonfiction books published in the educational field, including the Chelsea House book *Anwar Sadat* in the MAJOR WORLD LEADERS series. She has worked in education for 15 years and has traveled extensively throughout the world. After completing an educational project in Zimbabwe, Africa, she now lives in Glendale, California.

ARTHUR M. SCHLESINGER, JR. is the leading American historian of our time. He won the Pulitzer Prize for his book *The Age of Jackson* (1945) and again for a chronicle of the Kennedy administration, *A Thousand Days* (1965), which also won the National Book Award. Professor Schlesinger is the Albert Schweitzer Professor of the Humanities at the City University of New York and has been involved in several other Chelsea House projects, including the series REVOLUTIONARY WAR LEADERS, COLONIAL LEADERS, and YOUR GOVERNMENT.